NATO 2000

A Political Agenda for
a Political Alliance

BRASSEY'S ATLANTIC COMMENTARIES

Atlantic Commentaries present a series of introductory surveys of important issues affecting the Atlantic Alliance and its future. The booklets are written and edited with the general reader as well as the specialist in mind and are intended to provide insights into a number of different aspects of East–West and intra-Alliance relations. Among future topics planned are Spain's evolving role in European and transatlantic affairs; the role of NATO in the wider world; global security; and the interdependence of European, Japanese and United States security interests. Other subjects to be covered will include regional security issues, political and economic topics, country studies and future perspectives for international stability in the changing political environment of the 1990s.

Brassey's Atlantic Commentaries are produced in association with the NATO Information Service and various national Atlantic Committees or other associations and institutions concerned with different aspects of security. The opinions expressed are the responsibility of the editors and the contributors and do not necessarily represent the official views of NATO or of individual governments.

Brassey's Atlantic Commentaries

NATO's Defence of the North
Eric Grove

The Western European Union and NATO
Alfred Cahen

From Détente to Entente
Mark Eyskens

Titles of related interest from Brassey's

GROVE and WINDASS
The Crucible of Peace: Common Security in Europe

HANNING
NATO: Our Guarantee of Peace

GOLDSTEIN
Fighting Allies: Tensions within the Atlantic System

WINDASS
Avoiding Nuclear War: Common Security as a Strategy for the Defence of the West

BRASSEY'S ATLANTIC COMMENTARIES No. 3

NATO 2000

A Political Agenda for a Political Alliance

A15043 272077

JAMIE SHEA

Special Projects Officer
within NATO's Political Directorate

Edited by NICHOLAS SHERWEN

JX
1393
,N67
S54
1990
West

BRASSEY'S (UK)

A member of the Maxwell Pergamon Publishing Corporation

LONDON · OXFORD · WASHINGTON · NEW YORK · BEIJING
FRANKFURT · SÃO PAULO · SYDNEY · TOKYO · TORONTO

U.K. (Editorial)	Brassey's (UK) Ltd., 50 Fetter Lane, London EC4A 1AA, England
(Orders, all except North America)	Brassey's (UK) Ltd., Headington Hill Hall, Oxford OX3 0BW, England
USA (Editorial)	Brassey's (US) Inc., 8000 Westpark Drive, Fourth Floor, McLean, Virginia 22102, USA
(Orders, North America)	Brassey's (US) Inc., Front and Brown Streets, Riverside, New Jersey 08075, USA Tel (toll free): 800 257 5755
PEOPLE'S REPUBLIC OF CHINA	Pergamon Press, Room 4037, Qianmen Hotel, Beijing, People's Republic of China
FEDERAL REPUBLIC OF GERMANY	Pergamon Press GmbH, Hammerweg 6, D-6242 Kronberg, Federal Republic of Germany
BRAZIL	Pergamon Editora Ltda, Rua Eça de Queiros, 346, CEP 04011, Paraiso, São Paulo, Brazil
AUSTRALIA	Brassey's Australia Pty Ltd., PO Box 544, Potts Point, NSW 2011, Australia
JAPAN	Pergamon Press, 5th Floor, Matsuoka Central Building, 1-7-1 Nishishinjuku, Shinjuku-ku, Tokyo 160, Japan
CANADA	Pergamon Press Canada Ltd., Suite No. 271, 253 College Street, Toronto, Ontario, Canada M5T 1R5

Copyright © 1990 Brassey's (UK)

First edition 1990

Library of Congress Cataloging-in-Publication Data
Shea, Jamie
NATO 2000: a political agenda for a political alliance/Jamie Shea; edited by Nicholas Sherwen. — 1st ed.
p.   cm. — (Brassey's Atlantic commentaries; no. 3)
1. North Atlantic Treaty Organization.   2. North America—Foreign relations.   3. North America—Military policy.   4. Europe—Foreign relations.   5. Europe—Military policy.
I. Sherwen, Nicholas.   II. Title.   III. Title: NATO two thousand.   IV. Title: Political agenda for a political alliance.
V. Series.
JX1393.N67S54   1990   355'.031'091821—dc20
90-44025

British Library Cataloguing in Publication Data
Shea, Jamie
NATO 2000: a political agenda for a political alliance.—
(Brassey's Atlantic commentaries; no. 3).
1. North Atlantic Treaty Organization
I. Title II. Sherwen, Nicholas
355.031091821
ISBN 0-08-040727-7

Printed in Great Britain by BPCC Wheatons Ltd, Exeter

Contents

Editor's Note

NATO 2000 is published at a time when East–West relations are under-going the most far-reaching and largely unforeseen changes in the history of the post-war period. In focussing on the Alliance's political role in this period of transition, it seeks to dispel the notion that the fundamental *raison d'être* of NATO has disappeared. Always first and foremost a political Alliance, based on a transatlantic partnership which remains its single most important asset, NATO has for 40 years been the cornerstone of Western deterrence against a threat based on the vast military potential of Soviet Union and Warsaw Pact forces. Dependent on a strong military structure designed to contain that threat, the Alliance has thus became associated above all with the concept of sound defence and sufficient political solidarity to ward off other non-military forms of pressure.

That association tells only one part of the story. No less important now than at any stage in the past four decades, the military role of the Alliance can for the first time cede its place at the top of NATO's agenda to the realisation of the political goals which were always at the centre of the West's longer-term ambitions: the establishment of a new pattern of international relations in which ideological antagonism, backed by military might, can yield to cooperation, mutual confidence, and peaceful competition and a political environment in which human rights and political freedoms are guaranteed. It is thus not so much a question of the basis for the Alliance changing as it is a matter of correcting the perception that it was ever anything else.

NATO 2000 examines many of the elements involved in this funda-mental process of making progress towards long-standing goals. In Appendices I and II it casts an eye back to earlier initiatives to strengthen the concept of the Atlantic Community which remains central; and to translate into practical arrangements the logical integration of Europe's multifaceted defence structure into a coherent European defence com-munity. Both the 1962 Declaration of Paris and the 1952 Treaty establishing the European Defence Community speak for themselves. The text of the North Atlantic Treaty of 1949, the simplicity and brevity of which is in sharp contrast to the EDC Treaty, is included as Appendix III. Of course there are other essential differences between them. The EDC Treaty sought to create a supranational organisation. The North Atlantic Treaty brought into being an intergovernmental Alliance. The EDC Treaty was not ratified by two of the six signatory countries and was therefore never implemented. The North Atlantic Treaty was ratified and implemented and has earned its unique place in history. Now, as at the time when all these initiatives took place, the task of overcoming the unnatural division of Europe as a whole and of Germany in particular is pivotal. *NATO 2000* addresses this issue as well and includes at Appendix IV the text of a speech by Secretary General Wörner delivered to the Hamburg Overseas Club in February 1990. Following the first free elections to be held in the German Democratic Republic, few can doubt the accuracy of the analysis he offers here.

Since the book was written, two further developments of major importance have taken place. On 5 and 6 July 1990, the Heads of State and Government of NATO countries met in London and issued the London Declaration on a Transformed North Atlantic Alliance. The text of the Declaration has been added as Appendix V. And on 2 August 1990 Iraq invaded Kuwait, threatening the stability and security of the international situation. Both these events serve to underline the significance of the issues addressed in this Atlantic Commentary and the far-reaching nature of the challenges they represent.

About the Author

DR JAMIE SHEA obtained a first class degree in Modern History and French at the University of Sussex before going on to do his doctorate at Lincoln College, Oxford. He joined NATO in 1980 as a member of the Executive Secretariat of the North Atlantic Council and later joined the Political Affairs Division of the International Staff. For several years he was Head of NATO's Visits Section where he ran an extensive programme of visits and seminars catering for some 20,000 visitors to NATO each year. He now holds the post of Special Projects Officer within NATO's Political Directorate, writing extensively on Alliance issues and lecturing in Europe and North America on a regular basis.

Introduction

NATO is an Organisation which is not only capable of adapting to change but is leading the process of adaptation and setting the pace of the evolution taking place in Western attitudes to East–West relations. Despite occasional suggestions of atrophy, stagnation, determination to cling to the uncomfortable but at least predictable *status quo* of the Cold War era, and nostalgia for a tangible and identifiable military threat, the reality of the political process taking place within the Alliance is very different. From the standpoint of one who has worked within the structures of the Alliance for 17 years, it is in fact the freshness and vitality of the political life of NATO which are its saving graces. And the fact that despite the absence of a clear, simple structure for decision-making based, for example, on political bargaining between the member nations culminating in a majority vote, the Alliance works. Just how effectively would probably surprise the drafters of the 1949 Treaty more than anyone. In creating a system for transatlantic cooperation based on equal partnership, dependent on a sometimes mysterious and intangible process of reaching decisions by consensus and common accord, they must have entertained more than a few doubts about its viability. Their faith in the ability of governments to exploit the potential of the structure they proposed has been more than vindicated. A penetrating insight into this little-known but key aspect of NATO is to be found in a chapter written by the former Dean of the NATO Council, Belgian Ambassador André de Staercke ('An Alliance Clamouring to be Born – Anxious to Survive' in *NATO's Anxious Birth*. C. Hurst & Co, London 1985).

The Alliance's future, not its history, however, is the subject of this Atlantic Commentary. At the outset of the new decade the Alliance is facing the most fundamental alteration of the environment within which it has to operate in the entire 40-year history of the post-war period. How responsive can it be to the new demands and how versatile can it be in adapting to the unprecedented changes which are, by any yardstick partly the measure and consequence of its own success?

NATO faces a two-fold challenge: first, to develop its leading role in providing for change with stability. These are not necessarily synonymous. Both the fact and the prospect of fundamental reform in the Soviet Union and Central and Eastern European countries offer the possibility of changes in their relationships with the international community, the full implications of which have yet to be seen. They have certainly opened up a new and richer dialogue between East and West. The reality of confrontation has now hopefully moved aside to make way for practical cooperation in addressing global, as well as bilateral or regional, issues. But the bold course of Mr Gorbachev's reforms within the Soviet Union itself has led to new challenges which will not be easily resolved. The severity of the internal difficulties within the Soviet empire cannot be overstated. Some commentators have gone so far as to suggest that if the chapter on the post-war world has been closed, the next one could witness a disintegration of the political structures of the Soviet Union and Central and Eastern Europe which would pose a new threat to world peace.

NATO's second challenge is to correct the public image of an Organisation which has been, from the very outset, a political tool created for a political purpose enshrined in a political treaty. Current references to the need for NATO to become 'more political' express only half a truth. The fact is that throughout the post-war years, the Alliance has been distracted from its underlying political purpose by the paramount need to contain the implicit threat of a militarily unstable imbalance of forces which, as Moscow now admits, could not but give the NATO Allies legitimate concerns regarding Soviet intentions. The record clearly shows the crises that have passed, and the periods of increased tension which have been met with imperfect but sufficient political solidarity on the part of the West to cause them to recede. What the record does not show are the many crises which have not occurred, nor the occasional rise in tension which has been averted by the joint exercise of political restraint and Allied solidarity. In such circumstances the Treaty which holds the Alliance together has provided fixed points of reference in an uncertain world — a handrail up an obscure staircase, to which member countries have been able to cling without knowing exactly where the stairs would ultimately lead. How this double

challenge facing NATO can be met is explored in this Atlantic commentary. There are many questions to which there cannot as yet be firm
answers, but almost more important at this stage is to ensure that the
questions being posed are the right ones. We pose some of them here,
and suggest some of the likely responses to them.

The background to the current intensive debate on the role and scope
of the Alliance is of course the extraordinary scale and potential im-
plication of the revolution in ideas and conceptual analysis which pertain
to the international developments of the last year. From the repression
of political freedoms and of an embryonic democratic movement in
China in June 1989, we had moved by February 1990 to the formal
abandonment of single-party systems in the very heartland of Marxist-
Leninist ideology. As a consequence, a new wind blows through international relations, leaving in its wake promise and hope as well as a
degree of chaos. No part of the *modus vivendi* under which the international community has operated for the past three to four decades has
been left untouched. It is, nevertheless, in the fulcrum of the Soviet
Union and Eastern Europe where the heat is at its most intense. The
clamour for self-determination, political and religious freedoms, human
rights, and democracy is drowning out the cries for reform within the
old system and assuming a momentum which renders pleas for caution
and a planned approach all but inaudible. The immensity of the task
which Mr Gorbachev has set himself is even more significant when it
is understood that in creating an environment in which change could
take place, he has consciously had to foster a climate of instability,
knowing that it is both a prerequisite for, and a threat to, his grander
designs.

Riding high on a tide of political and economic reform, Central and
Eastern Europe has thus undergone a political metamorphosis — a process as yet incomplete, sometimes perilously close to reversal or sudden
extinction, yet holding on by sheer determination to the one ingredient
which the communist dream has failed to provide — genuine hope.

Perhaps the most striking feature of the change in the situation of
Central and Eastern Europe, and the resulting hiatus in the entire
East–West relationship, is its whirlwind speed. The countries of Europe
and their North American counterparts are within six short months
contemplating revolutions in their political thinking and in their external

policies which nothing short of finding themselves suddenly and unexpectedly at war could have inspired in former times. New policies are being formulated in the West even as the changes are occurring in the East. Before the dust settles on this uncharted and unexplored terrain, budgets are being redrafted and long-term decisions contemplated which may not have time to be implemented before another series of upheavals intervenes.

To establish fixed points of reference in all this and to distinguish between the permanent features of the new Europe and those which are merely symptoms of further change, is the stuff of science fiction. The tangible and irrefutable fact, however, is that the incoming tide has attacked the sandcastle standing at the shoreline and washed away any semblance of permanence it might have had. The foundations of the edifice were built on the illusion that one-party domination of the nation-state by repressive structures can provide a lasting system. It cannot. When its walls begin to crumble the ensuing demolition may be over in a few seconds.

In the meantime, international political developments do not stand and wait. The new *détente* between East and West has raised issues which need to be addressed in the short-term however incomplete may be the process which is bringing them about. One such issue, not unnaturally, is the role of the North Atlantic Alliance and the underlying partnership between Europe and North America which is its single most important asset. To what extent is the involvement of the United States in European security and stability still needed? Can the Alliance adapt to the new situation and still perform a useful role? Have other institutions the potential to take over its functions successfully?

This Commentary seeks to pose some of the questions and to chart some of the possible answers. First, by discussing what NATO is already doing to establish the political agenda for the next decade; and second, by examining what the 16 nation Alliance could do to enhance further its political role and coordinate Western efforts to ensure a peaceful and stable environment in which the transition from East–West confrontation to East–West cooperation can take place. Against this background the Commentary inevitably leaves major questions unanswered. Will the Soviet Union itself survive in anything resembling its present form? Has '*perestroika*' led, in the language of one Soviet commentator, to '*catastroika*' and the disintegration of Soviet society with all its attendant risks of civil unrest and internal conflict? And, if so, how long before such conflict becomes external, with forces of nationalism, ideology and religion in more or less violent opposition across as yet undrawn frontiers?

What seems certain is that the most dangerous course is that which is dictated by inaction. As history has so often demonstrated, it is the void which creates the conditions for repressive forces to flourish. And while the Soviet Union grapples with its destiny and the countries of Central and Eastern Europe, freed from the shackles of the Brezhnev Doctrine, strike out on their own, the Alliance has no more pressing mandate than to ensure that the process takes place in as stable an international environment as possible. This may mean accepting structural change and re-thinking its strategy for peace. It may mean discarding some of the most cherished tenets of post-World War II political theology. But it definitely does not mean unravelling the strands of transatlantic cooperation and dialogue which have provided the world with the basic guarantees on which peaceful development has heavily depended for the past forty years.

More than once in the history of the post-World War II environment there have, in fact, been calls for the contractual relationship between Europe and North America, established by the 1949 Treaty, to be strengthened and deepened by a clearly identifiable Atlantic Community of interests and ideals. At a time when the community of interests between the two sides of the Atlantic is again assuming such importance, this Commentary also examines the possible forms of institutionalised arrangements which might be introduced to give a new structure to this all-important dialogue. The subject is indeed not a new one. In 1962 a little known document called the Declaration of Paris, issued by some 90 eminent political thinkers, drawn from the then 15 members of the Alliance, put forward a series of practical measures which could be taken to reinforce the transatlantic relationship. The text of that declaration is reproduced here in full. Some of its ideas have been overtaken by events. The Alliance has, for example, a dynamic and effective system for consultation on the role of nuclear weapons within the defence and deterrence structure. The recommendation that such a system should be created is, therefore, no longer of relevance. Other sections of the

Declaration, however, relate to aspects of the transatlantic relationship which are as current issues of concern now as they were at the time they were drafted.

If the present discussion of the future of the transatlantic relationship finds an echo in the 1962 Declaration of Paris, so movement towards the creation of a Western European security concept or 'European defence identity' has its own historical roots. The debate on the 'European Defence Community' (EDC), which came so close to creating a European army and with it a European foreign policy dimension until rejected by the French National Assembly in 1954, is another remarkable example of the pendulum theory of political evolution.

Readers not familiar with the EDC debate may find other parallels with the present-day discussion — not least the focus on the future of a united Germany in the security structure of Europe. The text of the unratified EDC Treaty is reproduced at Appendix II (together with an historical note on the origins of the EDC).

The first task facing the Alliance is thus to establish its political agenda on at least three fronts: its role in setting out the parameters of the East–West relationship; its management of the transatlantic relationship and the development, if needed, of the Atlantic Community of interests; and the clarification of the European security dimension and its relationship with the overall East–West and transatlantic evolutionary process.

The Alliance's second task is undoubtedly to convey to public opinion an accurate picture of what its role has been, what it is now and potentially, what it may become.

Popular images of the North Atlantic Alliance, and particularly of its organisational structures, have seldom had much to do with the reality. Both in its treaty language and in its implementation, NATO has always been intrinsically political in nature and aspirations, even if, repeatedly, it has had to subjugate its longer-term political objectives to the immediate requirements of security. When some adjustment of priorities did appear possible, as in 1956, 1968 and 1979, a Hungary, a Czechoslovakia or an Afghanistan set the clock back. Now, for the first time, there is a sufficient basis for reinstating NATO's political role at the top of the Alliance's agenda for the 1990s, where it belongs.

Three notions characterise the past and future political identity of the

Alliance. First, the juridical basis of the North Atlantic Treaty, Article 51 of the United Nations Charter. If the legitimacy of the transatlantic security partnership were on trial, there could be no better witness for the defence than the United Nations and its tacit recognition of its own limitations in terms of providing protection for the territorial integrity of its members and preserving their right of self-determination. Second, the transatlantic partnership itself, in the manner of its evolution, provides ample evidence that the real basis for the North Atlantic Treaty does indeed lie in the community of interests between the European and North American members of the Alliance and not in any selfless or magnanimous gestures on the part of the United States and Canada towards a Europe in which they have no direct or vital stake. And third, the linkage between the objectives of the Alliance and the whole process known as the CSCE is such that the political credentials of NATO in the intensely political struggle for freedom, openness, democratic ideals and human rights throughout Europe are well established. For those who tend to question the Alliance member countries' intense concern with respect for these principles, and their right to challenge governments which infringe them, it is worth recalling that there has been no greater impediment to international confidence and thus to security and cooperation than the failure of the Soviet Union to apply them to its own citizens and allies.

For all that, while the political identity of NATO may not change, its public image must certainly begin to reflect far more accurately what its past and present roles have been and what it can offer in the future. Events are moving fast, and despite the fact that changes in East–West relations and in Eastern Europe are still in their infancy, policies are being formulated and assumptions made which appear to take little account of those realities which have not changed, and probably cannot change in the short-term. First, the establishment of democratic societies and pluralist political systems (not necessarily on purely Western European models) through free elections, the permanent safeguarding of the right of self-determination, and guaranteed protection of human rights, are not yet *faits accomplis*, nor can they become so overnight. They each depend, ultimately, not only on the physical supports of a social and political structure which allows them to thrive but also on the moral supports of a tradition and a code of practice which may take many years to develop. And second, the Soviet Union, deprived of its hegemonic control over Central and Eastern Europe, perhaps disarmed by international treaty to the tune of over 50 per cent of its armed manpower and equipment in Europe, and turned in on itself, while it battles with internal political and economic difficulties, will remain the dominant political and military presence on the European continent.

If the Soviet Union comes through its present crises and begins to resolve its economic difficulties, that presence becomes still more significant, regardless of ideological or other ambitions. The size of the Soviet Union, perhaps less a republic or two, in relation to that of the European land mass as a whole, will continue to be the single most important geo-strategic fact of European life.

In this situation there is no shortage of material for debating the future of alliances; the need for change; the creation of better structures to address the presumed new line-up of international allegiances and co-operative endeavours. The future of the transatlantic relationship is high on the agenda. James Baker, the United States Secretary of State, has proposed measures to strengthen the EC–US relationship. The British Foreign Secretary, Douglas Hurd, has added his voice to the call for a new European architecture which would, among other goals, permit a 'deepening and broadening' of the transatlantic partnership. Others have spoken of the emergence of a 'New Atlantic consensus'. Whether to consolidate the latter or to give it a better focus, NATO's former Secretary General, Lord Carrington, has suggested the creation of a new body in which each Alliance country would be represented at the level of Deputy Foreign Minister with the 'political clout, impetus and sense of urgency' which are now 'vital'. Outside the Alliance, there are other clubs and institutions in plentiful supply which can lay claim to different sections of the jigsaw.

Like the pieces of the puzzle itself, their edges overlap and interlock according to a complex pattern which you can learn only by picking up the pieces and trying to make them fit. The changing East–West relationship at the centre of the picture may be clear enough and the pieces of that can be picked out quite easily but there are large expanses of difficult sky and sea which are nothing like so easy to discern — the future of European integration, the role of European Political

Cooperation, the Western European Union (WEU), the Independent European Planning Group (IEPG), the European Free Trade Area (EFTA), the Helksinki process, bilateral relationships, the neutrals and non-aligned, the new group of 24 operating under the aegis of the EC to coordinate economic aid for Eastern Europe, and so on. And when we think we've finished the puzzle, there is the inevitable piece missing, or the one that does not belong anywhere. Where is that elusive European political unity? And where does Mr Gorbachev's 'Common European Home' fit into the overall picture?

In Atlantic Commentary No. 3 no attempt is made to trace a path through the whole wilderness. The focus is on the role and relevance of the Atlantic Alliance itself and on the notion of a revitalised Atlantic Community. 'NATO's Next Decade': A Political Agenda for a Political Alliance' looks at assumptions which are currently being made and finds some of them faulty. It looks at the rule-book with the critical eye of a practised observer of NATO's policy formulation process and acknowledges that parts of it need to be re-written. And it points out the dangers of assuming that because there is a change of players, introduction of new rules, a different angle of the field, and a touchline further back from the action, the goal posts have also moved. In terms of East–West relations they, of course, remain where they were.

Historians may be tempted to reverse their traditional role and redraw the political map of Europe in anticipation, but the reality is that none of the recent events in Europe alter the basic condition for progress to which the Alliance has been wedded from the beginning: the capability to resist the use of a military force or political pressure by a Soviet Union with a capability to decide to chance its hand by bringing those pieces into play and perhaps, in less happy times, desperate enough to risk all by doing so. It is, after all, many years since any serious political analyst predicted an imminent invasion of Western Europe or a Soviet strategic attack on North America. They have merely stated that the capability for either of these exists, examples of a willingness to resort to force abound, and ideological aims provided a pretext if ever one was needed. There are good reasons for supposing that neither of the latter has much relevance today, although they could do so again at some future date. However, the capabilities and the risks remain.

Central to the complex debate of the future of East–West relations and the transition from the stagnation of Cold War confrontation to a new era of constructive dialogue and cooperation, is the role of Germany. Geographically, economically and politically the heartland of the European continent, Germany cannot but be the queen on the political chess board. The familiar divided Europe containing a divided Germany may have suggested checkmate between East and West but the underlying assumption has always been that there would again be movement when the time was ripe. That time has come. The path has been long and arduous. From the early days of the division, reluctance to contemplate any move which might render it permanent led to the use of language reflecting a grudging pragmatism: the 'so-called German Democratic Republic' existed but was only recognised at first by the Soviet Union and its dependent satellite states. We moved on, and in time even within the Federal Republic calls for reunification became linked with a slightly quaint fringe of German public opinion unable to adapt to the new reality. Now the language has changed again. 'Unification' not 'reunification' is the order of the day, thus side-stepping the suggestion that the process might result in attempts to return to pre-war borders. Throughout this period, and in particular since the erection of the Berlin Wall, the Alliance has stuck doggedly to its position that the Four Power status of Berlin and the agreements relating to it must be upheld and has reiterated again and again its concern that the status of Berlin must not be challenged. Beyond that, the question of relations between the two Germanies was largely an internal matter. Improvements were welcomed when they occurred. Moral support to the Federal Republic was offered when the temperature cooled and when border restrictions and obstructions were used by the East to increase the pressure. The Federal Republic did better than survive this period and came out of it with all its limbs intact, without ever having to 'internationalise' the problem more than was already the case under treaty terms. The question of unification was thus never formally on the Alliance's political agenda, even though it remained an explicit Alliance goal formally agreed by all the Allies when the Federal Republic joined NATO in 1955.

That time has passed and in a speech delivered in Hamburg on 8 February 1990, NATO's Secretary General placed 'The Atlantic Alliance and German Unity' squarely at the centre of his own agenda for the Alliance's future. The text of his speech is reproduced here at Appendix IV.

At no stage in the last four decades have circumstances combined to produce a more urgent requirement for the facts of international political life to be recognised. It is in this perspective that the interests of peaceful evolution can best be served by a combination of imaginative thinking and a willingness to explore the lessons of history in full before rejecting them as irrelevant. In this Commentary we have tried to provide samples of both of these components of progress.

Information Directorate NATO   Nicholas Sherwen
April 1990

NATO's Next Decade: A Political Agenda for a Political Alliance

JAMIE SHEA

Managing change: will NATO be up to the job?

The 50th Anniversary of NATO will coincide with the end of the 20th century. Already the 21st century looms on the horizon and policy-makers are asking themselves how the Alliance can be adapted to meet the opportunities and challenges of the 1990s. These are rapidly being determined. The final years of the 1980s have seen rapid and un-precedented change in East–West relations. The old and familiar reference points of a politically divided Europe and of the Cold War have all but disappeared. With them have gone many of the planning assumptions on which Western defence policy has been based for 40 years. There are now more variables than constants and one British Member of Parliament, paraphrasing the celebrated novel by Tom Wolfe, has spoken of 'the bonfire of the certainties'. In their place we have a world of movement and of uncertainty. The Alliance views this new dynamic environment with a mixture of satisfaction and trepidation. On the one hand, it believes that its own cohesion and resolve through-out 40 long years of containment must have something to do with the mellowing of the Soviet and East European system; on the other hand, it realises that the current changes in East–West relations will pace immense new demands and political tasks upon it. Will NATO be up to the job? Managing an established order and smoothing down its rough edges is one thing; creating a new and better international order, without losing its sense of purpose and internal cohesion in the process, is an altogether different enterprise.

For the past 20 years, the Alliance has had a roadmap through the tangled web of East–West relations. It is known as the Harmel Doctrine, after the Belgian Foreign Minister who, in 1967, lent his name to the report on the future tasks of the Alliance. Alliance watchers will be familiar with its outlines. It advocates a balanced strategy of defence and deterrence, on the one hand; dialogue and *détente* on the other. The function of the Harmel Doctrine was not so much to transform the political map of Europe as to stabilise it. Continued defence efforts would provide a framework of order and predictability in which the East–West political dialogue would evolve; this dialogue in turn would attenuate hostility and misunderstanding so that the military balance would, over time, reflect a common East–West concept of security — one that would be reassuring and even cooperative rather than threatening and accident-prone. Harmel thus became a formula for slow political change in Europe within the existing bloc structures; or, if one prefers, a recognition that the *status quo* would probably last for a very long time, so that the function of *détente* was to make that *status quo* as relaxed and as tolerable as possible.

NATO's dual Harmel strategy was an instrument of security and *détente* rather than a radical blueprint for the future of Europe designed to challenge the *status quo* head on. Success lay in performing well the delicate balancing act between the two poles of dialogue and defence, in making them mutually supportive rather than mutually antagonistic. In 1967, with *détente* fragile and tension very much in the air, the techniques of safeguarding stability appeared more important than ultimate political objectives. Yet this familiar, if somewhat frustrating, situation for the Alliance has been disrupted by the arrival of Mr Gorbachev in the Kremlin. Within five years, which represents the design phase of a modern motor vehicle, change of the sort that we would have expected to happen slowly — in our best scenario over decades — has actually taken place.

The momentum of change

It is not merely the scope but also the speed of change that has proved overwhelming, undermining along the way all preconceived Western notions of how change, once it began, would proceed. Many believed it would come by popular explosion: in fact so far, and with the notable exception of Romania and the militant nationalist forces carrying out their own struggle within the Soviet Union itself, it has happened peacefully and largely with the active prompting or the passive connivance of the Communist authorities. Others held that change would come in Central and Eastern Europe first and only later inside the Soviet Union, which would attempt either to halt or delay such a process: the opposite has proved true. Many experts argued that Moscow would tolerate reform in Hungary or Poland only because these two nations had traditionally been allowed more latitude in their internal economic arrangements than their neighbours. After all did not 'goulash communism' and Solidarity pre-date Gorbachev's arrival in power? Yet it was clearly not the Soviet intention to sandwich a reformist Poland between itself and neo-Stalinist régimes in East Germany or Czechoslovakia. Despite a standard of living and a security system that appeared to anchor their authority, these two have now been swept away as well. In their case not in a matter of years, or slowly, as in Poland or Hungary, but in weeks or even days, so powerful has been the acceleration of history. The process of change has acquired a self-sustaining momentum that, if started by the Soviet leadership, has now taken it far beyond its control. Western observers worrying anxiously about the newly-drawn boundaries of the Brezhnev Doctrine have had increasingly to confront the evidence that no limits exist any longer, making a post-imperial Soviet system rather like the West: as much an observer as an actor in a process that will determine its future.

Towards the end of 1989 there was much hyperbolic talk of 'the end of history' or 'the end of ideology'. This was perhaps understandable. It was a landmark year in East–West relations. It witnessed the collapse of no less than six Communist régimes in Central and Eastern Europe, all but one in relatively peaceful circumstances. Today only Albania remains as the standard-bearer of the traditional orthodoxy, but for how much longer? The scope of change was matched only by its suddenness: Communism had always seemed the most robust of ideologies, with the police state and the egalitarian ideal combining to ensure a degree of internal cohesion and external solidarity. Yet here was a system that previously had been prepared to go to almost any length to impose itself, suddenly volunteering to share power or give it up altogether. Europe, as a result, is currently experiencing the third major reordering of its states system this century, but this time without the trigger of social collapse that was previously furnished by either war or revolution.

The challenge to liberal democracy

Some, like President Mitterrand, have drawn the parallel with 1789 and the word 'revolution' has been used frequently in conjunction with the upheaval and transition that Central and Eastern Europe are currently experiencing. In reality we are witnessing more of a 'counter-revolution' as the countries of this region attempt to shake off the alien mould of the past 40 years and re-affirm their national specificities. For them history and thus true ideological debate are only just beginning, for they are looking to rediscover a lost past as much as to embrace a new future. By comparison, it is the rest of Europe which is truly revolutionary and internationalist at the present times as the European Community embarks on monetary union, seeks to complete the internal market of 1993 and draws into closer association the EFTA countries. Moreover, the new street revolutionaries of the Communist world have on the whole been eminently reasonable and pragmatic in their de- mands — tolerating for the time being a continued rôle for Communists in government, focussing more on the abuses of power of the old guard rather than on the existence of the old guard itself, and seeking changes to the Warsaw Treaty Organisation in a way that is calculated not to upset Moscow through over-hasty moves towards neutrality. A revolu- tion presupposes a complete change not only of régime but also of the social system. This is far from being the case in Central and Eastern Europe at the present time where the old value system and the new overlap or co-exist as uneasy bedfellows. As a result we can say with confidence that 1989 was the end of a particular phase of European history characterised by competition *in the international domain* between liberal democracy and collectivism. But such competition will un- doubtedly intensify *within individual nations*, particularly as far as the post-communist order in Central and Eastern Europe is concerned. It is thus pointless to argue that one ideology has 'won' and another has 'lost'. If anything, the experience of historical transition is likely to revitalise 'socialism with a human face' while placing new demands on neo-liberal democracies.

In the first place, as Francis Fukuyama pointed out in a less quoted section of his celebrated article, *The End of History*, if liberal democracy has declared itself not only the best but also the only conceivable system, it will no longer be able to justify its inadequacies by reference to an inferior, ailing rival. Greater expectations will inevitably arise, both within existing neo-liberal systems and among those on the outside who aspire to the economic benefits of the market economies. The West will correspondingly come under the double strain of attempting to over-come its own societal imperfections — drugs, environmental damage, industrial obsolescence — while being appealed to to combat these prob-lems on an even vaster scale in Central and Eastern Europe and the Third World. These expectations are based largely on the 'peace dividend', the hope that savings from a diminishing military competi-tion can be directed towards domestic priorities. The question in this respect is to what extent the Western nations have been involved in international affairs largely on account of the security threat arising from the East–West ideological confrontation. If so, will they remain engaged even in its absence, and be prepared tomorrow to work in the new, constructive international agenda (Third World debt, hunger, pollu-tion, population) with the same zeal that they devoted yesterday to the tasks of containment and military balance? This is especially pertinent in the case of the United States where historically internationalism has relied on a strong sense of external and ideological threat as counter-weight to isolationism.

The debate is already well-launched in the developing countries. On the one hand, they rejoice that the East–West struggle will no longer exacerbate their already considerable internal difficulties; on the other hand, they fear that they will suffer from a loss of interest by the in-dustrialised world now that they have less importance as pawns on a chessboard. In particular, they fear the new focus of the West, and especially of Western Europe, on the task of reconstruction in Central and Eastern Europe with its attendant redirection of resources. For instance, the President of the European Commission, Jacques Delors, has advocated a major increase in European Community aid to Central and Eastern Europe to the tune of US $23 billion per annum. This contrasts with the recently concluded Lome IV agreement between the Community and the African, Caribbean and Pacific (ACP) countries that offered the latter only US $14 billion over five years; in other words just over half of what Delors wishes the EC to spend in Central and Eastern Europe in a single year.

Many commentators have presented the mainsprings of historical change in Europe in purely economic terms. Certainly the economic gap between East and West has widened considerably in the 1980s. The people of Central and Eastern Europe have become increasingly frustrated at being reduced to the second class citizens of the continent and embittered that it should be the system not they which is to blame for their lower living standards. No-one would deny that communism, although successful initially at promoting rapid industrialisation and resource mobilisation, has proved increasingly incapable of addressing, let alone solving, the problems of modern post-industrial societies. Its emphasis on massive levels of growth and the liberal use of raw materials and resources has indeed made it, historically, into a caricatural form of capitalism. It has thus fallen foul of the third industrial revolution of information technologies with its emphasis on intensification rather than expansion, decentralised decision-making, energy saving, environ-mental protection and rapid innovation at the grassroots. Yet the economic failure of communism has provoked not so much a comparison with a more prosperous West as with living standards at home that have significantly retrogressed in the 1980s. The worsening supply situation, massive price increases and rapidly devaluing currencies have brought about the paradox that communism has no longer been able to provide socialism. The question thus arises as to whether the peoples of Central and Eastern Europe wish to embrace neo-liberalism or simply rescue socialism through the selected and limited importation of Western-style market mechanisms. In such a perspective, change in Central and Eastern Europe represents less the triumph of neo-liberalism as an economic model to be admired and copied than a revival of the notion of a 'third way' between liberalism and collectivism that exercised intellectuals so much in the 1960s.

If one can speak of liberal democracy as having triumphed, this is less because of any specific economic or societal model that it is supposed to reflect than because it has on the whole made a better job than

communism at upholding universal values. In the past the East would
contrast 'bourgeois' values based on the rights of the individual with
'collectivist' values, such as the right to work, to be housed, and so on.
Yet its miserable economic performance in recent times has devalued
these benefits by comparison with the opportunities afforded by individual freedom. Thus Gorbachev in his milestone speech to the United
Nations in December 1988 endorsed these universal values as the indispensable basis for a revitalised socialism. By 'universal values' we
specifically mean those rights that are laid out in the United Nations
Declaration on Human Rights and the 1975 Helsinki Final Act of the
Conference on Security and Cooperation in Europe: openness, political
pluralism, free elections, freedom of travel, speech and of organisation.
If anything this is also what we generally mean by the 'Western model'
as such a concept can hardly be said to exist in the economic and societal
spheres where we have, at a given time, 'Reaganomics' in the United
States, Thatcherism in Britain, the French 'plan', German worker co-
management and the Scandinavian consensus around social democracy.
Thus the structure of Western human values is both universal and
permanent, while other values, particularly economic and societal, are
transient. The ideological failure of communism is due in no small part to
Marxism's attempt to relativise individual rights while granting absolute
value status to a specific and historically-determined economic model.

Influencing events

If the West, like the Soviet Union, cannot control the pace and direction of events, it is certainly in its interest to influence them. It cannot
be the aim of any Alliance policy to trust to the inherent dynamic of
change nor to follow Willi Brandt's advice and leave all 'to the
imagination of history'. The task for NATO is thus to be ready to
respond rapidly to new opportunities but in the meantime to take a
second look at the Harmel Doctrine. This is no longer just a means
of keeping open channels of communication in East–West relations but
the basis for a far-reaching policy for managing the dynamics of change,
not with a view to blunting them, but to the extent possible to steer
them towards specific political objectives. This is not to be confused
with the imposition of Western values in an attempt to produce a carbon

copy Western society in Eastern Europe. Such a goal would be futile
and misguided, but nor can the Alliance afford to be a passive spectator
of events. If it contented itself with no more than that, at best it would
lose a historic opportunity to permanently reshape East–West relations
into a new framework of cooperation; at worst, it would allow upheavals
and convulsions to occur in the East that would rebound against
Western defence and security.

The establishment of NATO in 1949 was an act of Western statesmanship. In the face of a clear ideological challenge from the Soviet
Union, based as much on political intimidation within West European
domestic politics as on military pressure from the Red Army, a small
group of far-sighted officials convinced their often reluctant administra-
tions to try a new experiment in international cooperation. To read the
history of the negotiations that led to the Washington Treaty of 1949
is to realise what a difficult birth NATO had.* In many countries
public opinion was hostile to the idea of an entangling politico-military
alliance, particularly one directed at yesterday's ally. Governments were
aware of the reversal of their national foreign policies that Alliance
membership would mean; equally they disagreed as to the extent of the
Soviet challenge and the most appropriate means of meeting it. George
Kennan, the American father of containment, later argued in this respect
that he opposed NATO because he believed the military consolidation
of the West would delay rather than hasten the overcoming of the division
of Europe. The Alliance came about because of the escalating pressure
of events on the outside, and the skilled manoeuvrings of the treaty drafters
on the inside who used these events to create consensus around the idea
of a transatlantic partnership founded on mutual interest.

It is worth recalling the circumstances of 40 years ago because the
dimensions of the challenge NATO faces today, if not its precise nature,
are similar. NATO policy makers also now have to create a new international order out of the débris of the old. They too are aware of the
inevitable passing of the old order while not yet being able to make out
the contours of the new as it emerges in the distance. They, like their

*See *NATO's Anxious Birth: the Prophetic Version of the 1940's*, by A. de Staercke &
others (C. Hurst & Co. London 1985).
Forging the Alliance, by Don Cook (Secker & Warburg. London 1989. Arbor House/
William Morrow. New York 1989).

predecessors in 1949, are conscious of the great stakes involved. There are historic opportunities to be seized while they are there; these opportunities call for new ideas and bold, imaginative action. But there are also risks involved for real change by definition cannot be smooth or automatic. A degree of instability is an inevitable by-product that has to be minimised even if it cannot be altogether avoided. To put it another way: the Alliance has to preserve stability in the short term in order to manage the change that is essential for stability in the long term. The risks can be greater if policies to exploit the opportunities turn out badly. So today's NATO leaders have, as never before, to combine prudence with imagination. Seeing only the opportunities without the risks, or the risks without the opportunities, is the surest recipe for failure. Both must be kept in a balanced perspective, at the very least during the next five years when the impact of change coming on top of years of stagnation is at its most dramatic, and a whole range of scenarios — running from optimal to worst-case — still all have an equal factor of probability. The biggest mistake the West could make would be to judge a single scenario the most probable just because it happens to be the most desirable. The present generation of NATO leaders have to meet our challenge in our circumstances to the same extent that their predecessors were able to meet their challenge in their circumstances 40 years ago. The environment is of course totally different but the conditions of statesmanship are the same: favourable historical circumstances and a proactive, ambitious policy able to impose a conceptual architecture on change that will give it meaning and progressively shape its outcome.

To address the first condition first: favourable historical circumstances. These the West clearly has in abundance. The East today is turning to the West. Its leaders acknowledge that the problems of communism are more than a temporary inconvenience. It has failed, and thus cannot be revived by selective tinkering. If a vaguely defined concept of 'socialism' is to be salvaged from the wreckage, as Mr Gorbachev and many of his colleagues proclaim, this can only be through the root and branch transformation of both political and economic structures. In other words, Communist leaders have publicly acknowledged that the ideology, Marxist-Leninism, and its practice, centralised control, provide no answers to the problems of societies seeking to move into the post-industrial age. They must turn to Western concepts for their inspiration. For Mr Gorbachev this would seem to mean two things: first, that if he repudiates neo-liberalism, he at least accepts that a successful socialist model must be open, pluralist and with a high degree of market mechanisms; second, that even differing socio-economic systems must be governed at the global level by a common set of universal values. Mr Gorbachev's language in this respect has become increasingly Western in its emphasis on economic inter-dependence, the renunciation of the use of force as an instrument of international diplomacy and East–West cooperation on global issues such as the environment, energy shortage, drugs, debt relief, hunger and over-population. This linguistic stridency shields a more funda-mental reality: that the Soviet Union and its reforming partners in Eastern Europe recognise that they cannot succeed by their own methods alone. While Mr Lech Walesa has frankly told the Unites States Congress that Poland will sink without long-term Western aid and support, Mr Shevardnadze says only that such aid will merely accelerate a reform in the Soviet Union which Moscow can and will, if necessary, carry out using its own resources. Yet if the states of Central and Eastern Europe will disagree as to the type and amount of Western aid they require, they all acknowledge that Western technology does not work without Western ideas. We now have a Soviet leadership that, unlike its Communist and Tsarist predecessors, no longer wishes to import Western technology while holding Western values at arm's length. For some, such as the Poles and the Hungarians, Western values — democracy, market forces, economic integration — are the end to be pursued; the way to escape from socialism. For the Soviet Union, on the other hand, and perhaps also for some of the less reform-minded governments in Eastern Europe, these values are clearly not an end but the means to restore socialism. Thus, although we cannot yet predict the future shape of societies in Central and Eastern Europe, two things seem certain: that they will all be very different from one another, and that, whatever their ultimate orientation, they will each contain a sizeable proportion of political pluralism and the mixed economy. The rôle of Western financial and technological support will be to give these ideas time and space to gain a foothold.

Shortcomings of the Soviet system

Mr Gorbachev is not reforming his system out of deference to the West. His incentive comes not from a Pauline conversion to the wisdom of pluralism or the market economy — both notions have been dismissed by him — but from the precipitous decline of the Soviet model. *Glasnost* has brought a flurry of revelations, surprising even Western sovietologists, about how bad things really are: a budget deficit totalling 10 per cent of GNP in 1988 compared to 5 per cent at the worst point of the American budget deficit in the late 1980s; growth rates that have been little more than 1 per cent for the past decade — indeed in 1989 the Soviet Union recorded negative or reverse growth for the first time since the 1920s. As the Prime Minister, Nikolai Ryzhkov, acknowledged in his 'State of the Union' address to the Supreme Soviet in June 1989, 40 million people live in poverty even by Soviet standards (defined as having expendable incomes of less that US $1,500 per annum). Declining public health is reflected in the fact that every sixth hospital bed is in an institution with no running water; one in three Soviet hospitals has no indoor toilets; a 950 bed hospital receives an average one or two hypodermic needles a day. Half the schools have no central heating, running water or indoor toilets. Soviet citizens today have a worse diet than did Russians under Tsar Nicholas II in 1913. Then Russia was the world's largest food exporter. Now it is the largest importer. There are 24 million farmers in the Soviet Union, more than the industrialised West and Japan combined, but they deliver only 22 per cent of the Western output, and one-third of that is spoiled before it reaches market. Last summer saw the first, albeit minor, food riots in Moscow and on one day in 1989 the daily shipment of bread failed to come into Leningrad, a condition not experienced since the German siege in World War II. Along with the diminishing supply of consumer goods and rampant alcoholism (40,000 deaths a year) Soviet sociologists speak of rising infant mortality rates, the increase in diseases such as meningitis and reduced life expectancy. Large-scale strikes, such as the miners in the Donbass, Kuzbass and Vorkuta areas in 1989, serve to focus leadership attention on the shortages, but they further compress industrial production and, in creating the impression that certain powerful unions can win privileged treatment, only encourage others to be more radical.

These strikes also force the Soviet leadership to divert major hard currency reserves to the purchase of consumer goods abroad at the expense of much-needed investment in capital goods, infrastructure and technologies.

The shortcomings of the Soviet system have been manifest for some time. At the beginning of the 1980s, however, they suddenly came to a head, generating throughout the Communist world a sense of crisis. On the one hand was the fact that 5 per cent of Soviet GNP was going to support client states in the Third World; and yet Soviet Third World activism, while procuring no economic and few strategic benefits, provoked in the United States the return of a right-wing Republican administration determined to restore the military balance and give containment a more activist content. The Strategic Defence Initiative of President Reagan epitomised, perhaps more than anything else, Soviet concerns: that rather than attempt to restore the strategic balance in the old weaponry in which Moscow had a large and perhaps decisive advantage, the United States would simply re-invent the rules of the strategic game. A new defence concept based on futuristic electronics, in which software was more important than hardware, suddenly placed all the cards on the Western side. The Soviet Union was made aware of its technological backwardness. The very ambition of SDI was a symbol of the new Western confidence as it completed the first stage of its adaptation to the third industrial revolution, this time in information technologies, while the Soviet Union was still digesting the impact of the first. Soviet hostility to the Strategic Defence Initiative was motivated, of course, by the desire to maintain a military advantage. Yet Moscow in the longer term had two more important choices: either to try to block SDI in order to gain time to catch up, or to so change the ground rules of East–West relations that the Soviet Union would no longer have to anticipate or fear Western military competition. To do this, of course, Moscow would have to remove the source of that Western response, namely its own military power, particularly in the conventional area and in the massive overhang in Central Europe.

Developments on the domestic front seemed to be the very reflection of the Soviet Union's reversals in the international scene. Mr Brezhnev's carrot and stick approach instead of giving the Soviet Union unlimited access to the finance and technology of a compliant West only succeeded in drying up the sources of both. The SS20 deployments, conceived as the *pièce de résistance* in a policy of softening up the NATO Allies, produced exactly the opposite effect: counter-deployments of Cruise and Pershing missiles and a Western alliance, including France, more united in anti-Soviet solidarity than anything Moscow had had to contend with since the early 1960s. On the economic front too, a favourable situation seemed to turn sour overnight. A growth rate as high as six per cent in the mid-70s was based on high commodity and energy prices, particularly oil. This soon made up 70 per cent of Soviet hard currency earnings. This was a period in which the per capita income of the more successful Warsaw Pact economies was higher than many Western European nations, for instance, Greece and Portugal. It thus became fashionable for Western academics to speak of the 'convergence theory', for it seemed that the East would progressively become more capitalist — even if only at the level of 'state capitalism' — and the West would become more social democratic and collectivist. By the onset of the 1980s, however, the return of the neo-liberal, free enterprise culture to the West combined with the sudden fall in commodity prices combined once more to open up the economic gap between the two halves of Europe. The internal market of 1993 in Western Europe is often credited as the single most important factor behind this widening gap. In reality, however, it is less a cause than a symptom. For 1993 has been made possible only by the new technologies, increased intra-Community trade and higher growth rates that were already manifest before the European Commission launched its great enterprise.

   The downturn in the Soviet economy was apparent to the Soviet leadership well before Mr Gorbachev's arrival in power. Indeed, Yuri Andropov, during his brief interregnum, began to address it, if only at the level of measures to reinforce discipline and combat corruption. The genius of Mr Gorbachev has been to recognise that his country's problems are not simply the result of inadequate motivation or lax discipline. These exist because the economy, and indeed society at large, are structurally flawed. Mr Gorbachev has been like a man peeling an onion; with each departing layer he becomes aware that the roots of the problem lie deeper than he at first believed. It is the lucidity of his analysis and his evident willingness to take enormous risks in imposing radical solutions that testifies to his sincerity. No previous Soviet leader would have been prepared to accept the social convulsions that anything other than surface reform means; although Mr Gorbachev can always tell his opponents that to allow the problems to worsen would entail even greater convulsions in the long term. Moreover, although many of his initiatives correspond to the traditional top-down approach of Soviet and Tsarist reformers, they are also largely the product of popular expectations. Mr Gorbachev is the first Soviet leader to represent the new managerial and technocratic middle class that emerged during Brezhnev's time. Educated and informed, this class demands economic reform and democratisation not simply because they are desirable in themselves but because they can use them to assert their claims against the hordes of bureaucrats who owe their influence to loyalty alone. It is the impact of this nascent civil society in the Soviet Union, together with Mr Gorbachev's readiness to seek economic improvements above all through political and institutional change, that makes the present *détente* more solid and durable than the abortive experience of the 1970s.

That we live in a period of revolutionary change is no longer a matter for debate. It is a revolution unlike other revolutions in the past. At times of fundamental change, people are expected to be more apprehensive and fearful. Paradoxically, however, most people these days feel more secure. The latest Eurobarometer opinion poll conducted by the European Community indicates that Western Europeans have a very low expectation of trouble. In 1980, for instance, more than half of Europeans polled expected a turbulent future of international discord (53 per cent); 10 years later only 23 per cent are pessimistic. The number of respondents who see no danger of war has virtually tripled from 15 to 42 per cent. This change is the direct result of Mr Gorbachev's *détente* policies. What is new is the confluence between internal and external *détente*. In the past, the Soviet Union tended to open up abroad and crack down at home or crack down abroad and open up at home. When external *détente* was pursued, the *détente* process would quickly be frustrated because it would end by provoking internal tension between and within the Central and Eastern European countries. We have only to think of the suspicions aroused by Mr Dubcek's Prague Spring, not only in the Soviet Union but in East Germany or Czechoslovakia, or of the East German decision to close its border with Poland during

Solidarity's Gdansk agreements in August 1981. Today, on the other hand, the internal and external *détente* policies are reinforcing each other, so that the Soviet Union would have to risk simultaneous domestic, intra-WTO and East–West crises if it decided to reverse course. In fact, the pattern has been one of a domino theory in reverse, with knock-on effects that have been largely unintended. Take, for instance, Hungary opening its borders with Austria perhaps without realising but certainly without caring that such an action, in allowing 40,000 East Germans to flee, would bring about the collapse of the régime in East Berlin. Prior to this decision, only Romania had dared to defy internationalist solidarity within the WTO. The Hungarian decision, in that it involved the denunciation of a bilateral treaty with East Germany, set a new precedent: making good relations with the West worth provoking a crisis within the WTO. The ultimate paradox is that Ceaucescu was finally the victim of his own policy. In 1968 he condemned the Soviet invasion of Czechoslovakia. Yet 21 years later he condemned the Soviet Union for not invading Poland following the appointment of Mr Mazowiecki as Prime Minister. In the first case, Mr Ceaucescu rested his independence on national sovereignty; in the second case on Communist orthodoxy. In both, he was attempting to play off one set of powerful neighbours against another, and in the end his own repressed population exposed him.

Rivers of ink have already been expended on conjecture regarding Mr Gorbachev's ulterior motives. Does he wish to reform communism or abandon it altogether? Is he trying to revitalise the Soviet system to renew the struggle against the West on a better basis in the future? Has he accommodated himself to the reality of the Soviet Union's terminal decline as a superpower and ideological bloc leader? Is he seeking only a soft landing for his country in a new European political order stressing cooperation and peaceful competition instead of the old ideological and military hostility?

We do not, of course, have any reliable answers to these questions, even five years into Mr Gorbachev's rule. All the more so as Gorbachev himself does not seem to have any such grand design either. He may well prefer to define this in the light of the speed and progress of his reforms — although sooner or later the reform process, if continued, will reach a point where this fundamental orientation towards specific

goals will be inevitable. Certainly Gorbachev has learned his pragmatism
from bitter experience. When he came to power in March 1985 he was
fond of telling Western businessmen that in four years he would turn
the Soviet economy around. The Soviet Union at that time was one of
the few countries in the world where the top leadership obviously had
a more defective understanding of national realities than the average
shopper. Yet although Western analysts often criticise Gorbachev for
not having a clear plan — in contrast to the Poles and Hungarians who
have the Western model resolutely in mind — his pragmatism stems
from an acute dilemma that does not exist anywhere else in Central and
Eastern Europe, with the possible exception of Yugoslavia. If socialism
failed in the GDR, there was always the option of joining the Federal
Republic. Indeed the success of neo-liberalism in the Federal Republic
virtually guaranteed that socialism would fail in the GDR once the
Berlin Wall was removed. Poland, Hungary and Czechoslovakia however will still be cohesive nations without communism. Indeed one can
argue that the national reconciliation that is following the demise of
communism will make them even more cohesive. The Soviet Union,
on the other hand, lacks any other source of legitimacy except for communism. It possesses no national or federal institutions that can provide
an alternative focus of popular loyalty. Thus Gorbachev, unlike his
WTO allies, will not consolidate but fragment his multinational state
by moving too quickly in both word and deed away from communism.
This perhaps explains why Gorbachev was originally in the lead of
reform in 1985 to 1988 but in 1989 was overtaken by his Central
European allies. If the Soviet Union is subsequently left too far behind,
there is a danger that it may retrogress.

Western opportunities and dilemmas

What matters for the West is less this sort of long-term speculation
than to seize current opportunities while they are available. In other
words, Mr Gorbachev's ultimate master-plan is not of prime importance. What counts is the extent that his actions are compatible with
Alliance interests and objectives and what scope they offer for improving
East–West relations. It is clear that the current changes in Central and
Eastern Europe are sufficiently real to offer considerable scope for

constructive Western involvement. For if it is clear that Western financial and technical help will not bear fruit in the absence of dynamic reforming efforts by countries in this area, it is also true that such efforts must have Western help to get off the ground. A Western economic study, for instance, has shown that there is a minimal difference between the success of Soviet *perestroika* or its failure (1.6 per cent growth at worse, 2.3 per cent at best). Thus, without Western help, the Soviet Union is condemned to fall further behind the West.

Gorbachev's economic adviser and a deputy Prime Minister, Leonid Abalkin, has said that *perestroika* will not show results until 1995 at the earliest. Can popular frustrations be contained in the meantime? According to a Soviet poll, 84.4 per cent have no confidence in the future.

The whole of Central and Eastern Europe is today in an appalling social, economic and environmental mess. The East–West divide could potentially give way to a far more worrisome North–South divide. Poland now has a per capita GNP at the same level as Indonesia. Its pollution levels have reached alarming proportions with reduced life expectancy and mounting instances of deformed children and declining public health. Sweden has recently had to grant the equivalent of £30 million in immediate aid to Poland for the introduction of pollution control equipment; the money for this technology is lacking in a country that is desperate to maintain production rates in industries that use five times as much energy as their Western counterparts to produce a single ton of steel. The European Community has also had to intervene to clean up Polish rivers.

In both Poland and Hungary, massive levels of foreign debt (US $39 million in the case of Poland, US $21 billion in the case of Hungary — the highest per capita in the world) significantly hamper economic restructuring. As former Prime Minister Rakowski was fond of pointing out, Poland would not be in such severe straits had it not had to reimburse Western banks to the tune of US $12 billion in the 1980s. The Hungarian Prime Minister, Niklos Nemeth, has said that his country needs to borrow US $2.5–3 billion a year for debt service alone. Yet it cannot do this as long as it conducts fifty per cent of its trade with COMECON, in goods such as buses which are too low quality to sell in the West. According to a study by the Budapest Institute for Economic and Market Research, only one in three Hungarian enterprises would survive open competition with Western industry. US $8 billion in Western capital over the next five years is needed to remedy this situation. Lech Walesa's calculation for Poland was US $10 billion. Overall, the WTO countries account for only two per cent of world trade. Communism has so deformed the economic structures of Central and Eastern Europe that, in the absence of massive and sustained Western help, there is not a local remedy in sight that would prevent them from remaining parlous or even worsening over the next decade. Bronislav Geremek, President of the Solidarity group in parliament, has conceptualised the challenge in the following way: 'It is easy turning an aquarium into fish soup, but how does one turn fish soup back into an aquarium?' Whereas hundreds of books this century have been written on how to convert capitalism into socialism, almost none have appeared on the opposite theme.

This uncomforting truism has placed Western policy-makers in something of a dilemma. We wish to integrate the Soviet Union and its allies as far as possible into the world economy. Present Bush means this when he speaks of 'beyond containment', a theme first developed in his speech to the University of Texas A and M on 11 May 1989. Such integration will hasten the progress of *perestroika* by giving these countries access to all the benefits — financial, technical, managerial — of the advanced, industrial economies. It will also ideally foster ties of interdependence that will more or less lock the Soviet Union into the Western system and induce it to toe the line in its international behaviour. There is indeed a whole body of academic literature that encouragingly shows that wars between liberal, democratic countries are exceptionally rare. Yet it is easiest to achieve this integration when *perestroika* has succeeded; when, for instance, the Soviet Union has introduced a realistic pricing of goods, a convertible currency, private ownership, a stock and bond market and a Western-style banking system for handling investment, profits and currency flows. The problem is that without Western assistance the Soviet Union is hardly likely to be able to cross these individual Rubicons for fear of the social upheaval they are likely to cause. Already currency convertibility has been pushed back to around 1992 at the earliest. The depth of the Central and Eastern European political and economic crises obliges the West to adopt a multiple strategy.

Short-term aid and longer-term investment

First, an immediate injection of aid to enable these countries to survive the winter. Since the NATO 40th Anniversary Summit meeting
in May 1989, the West has finally agreed that Mr Gorbachev's reforms
are in the Western interest and must be supported. This meeting was
the catalyst for the first Western attempt at a coordinated package of
aid, the multiplier effect resulting not merely from an increase in aid
but also from that aid being targeted at the pressure points in the
economy: the supply situation and the debt repayment problem. Under
the auspices of the European Commission, 24 Western industrial nations
have since met on several occasions, including at Foreign Minister level,
to coordinate food aid for Poland, debt rescheduling for Poland and
Hungary, new stabilisation credits, and Western governmental backing
for an active interventionist policy by the International Monetary Fund
and other institutions. These measures give reforming régimes a breathing space. They help to cushion the impact of the hard economic
decisions bound up with reform, thus preserving popular support while
those decisions take effect. More importantly, this Western rescue
package has bolstered the domestic position of the reformers and
encouraged Eastern European governments in general to 'bite the
bullet' The West's wager in concentrating at first on Poland and
Hungary in the hope that this would apply indirect pressure on those
dragging their feet certainly seems to have paid off with East Germany
and Czechoslovakia now embarking on a similar reform programme.

This short-term programme of aid is, of course, the easiest way for
the NATO Allies to react to the changes in the East. It can be focussed
on the most visibly obvious requirements, is limited in scope, does not
involve an open-ended commitment and necessitates only the most
limited coordination among the donor countries. Yet if the East–West
economic division of Europe is to be overcome, the medium-term is
the most important. Central and Eastern Europe has to be able to stand
on its own two feet with industries able to compete in international
markets and populations content to remain at home and rebuild their
societies. Political reform is the easiest form of change. Western observers must not fall into the trap of thinking that free elections and representative parliaments will in themselves unleash a '*Wirtschaftswunder*'

throughout Central and Eastern Europe. There is no automatic connection between democracy and successful market economies — the one
inevitably giving rise to the other — just because this happens to be
the most prevalent model in the West. Certainly democratisation will
give economic reconstruction an enormous boost: it will enable more independent experts and technocrats to be recruited into non-Communist
or coalition governments, as in Poland; it will persuade the populations
that a little more belt-tightening in the cause of true reform is justified;
and, above all, it will induce the West to grant the aid that is needed
to 'pump prime' the reforms. Yet democratisation will be to no avail
if the breathing space it gives is not used to take the hard economic
decisions to move to a market economy: measures to combat inflation
(currently running at 1,000 per cent in Poland), to legalise private
property, to cut government subsidies on staple and consumer goods,
to make currencies convertible, and to offer Western investment
attractive conditions (ownership of industries, repatriation of profits,
etc.). In the absence of such a clear economic plan, as in the Soviet
Union, political freedom can well produce an unholy alliance between
conservatives and workers; the first resenting the loss of privileges, the
second the shortages and chaos that half-baked economic reforms will
be increasingly blamed for causing.

There has been much talk in the West of a new Marshall Plan for
Central and Eastern Europe. The idea was first proposed by the former
Italian Prime Minister, Ciracao da Mita. Although one can argue that
the package of support currently being put together by the West adds
up to the largest programme since Stalin forced Central and Eastern
Europe to reject Marshall aid in the late 1940s, it falls far short of the
dimensions of a modern-day Marshall Plan. American economists have
costed such a plan at (±) US $120 billion, although this can be only
the roughest of estimates. There are a number of arguments against such
a scheme. First, the shortage of capital in the West. The Bush administration, for instance, beset by budget and trade deficits, is already
having to earmark around US $50 billion for the rescue of the US savings
and loans banks. The recent turmoil in El Salvador, Panama, Nicaragua
and the Philippines has also brought it home to the Administration that
an economic stabilisation programme for these countries will soon be
urgent — whether to buttress nascent democracies or as a sweetener

to others to move in a democratic direction. Moreover, Marshall aid in the late 1940s was given to countries that already had democratic and market systems and which, through the Organisation for European Economic Cooperation (OEEC), were taking the first steps to integrate their economies and coordinate their production. Central and Eastern Europe is different: it is not integrating, as Western Europe finally completes this process in the Single Market in 1993, it is fragmenting. Current Soviet attempts to form a common market trading system in Central and Eastern Europe, as proposed by Prime Minister Ryzhkov to the Congress of People's Deputies in December 1989, would seem to be too little too late. Equally, Central and Eastern Europe does not have an unlimited capacity to absorb Western funds, particularly as the two most needy candidates, Poland and Hungary, already have massive external debts. A further problem with a massive infusion of funds is that it could well help discredited Communist régimes maintain themselves in power. Western policy must be to reconcile Communists to the inevitability of change, and their interest in a smooth transition. Neither we nor they wish to return to the situation of untied credits of the seventies that produced one year's feast followed by ten years' famine. This time round the choice must be made between 'guns and butter', and indeed the enormous defence budget reductions in Hungary and Poland (− 25 per cent) suggest that it is being made.

The economic problems of Central and Eastern Europe are such that Western governmental help, no matter how generous, is unlikely to be more than a drop in the ocean. Salvation must come in the form of the private sector. Where Western primary investment goes, sub-contractors, service industries, employee training and infrastructure will eventually follow. As an inducement, the Western governments can encourage joint ventures, lift tariff barriers on Eastern exports, guarantee in the short term Western venture capital, lift restrictions on the flow of technology and offer training for Eastern European managers and aspirant entrepreneurs. Indeed, in the wake of the EC Summit dinner in Paris on 18 November, and the United States–Soviet Malta summit, much of this is already happening. President Bush has granted Hungary and Poland most favoured trading nation status, COCOM is taking a fresh look at its 'blacklist' of prescribed technologies and President Mitterrand has proposed a Central and Eastern Europe investment bank with an initial capitalisation of US $11 billion. Senator Sam Nunn, Chairman of the United States Senate Armed Services Committee, has proposed that American banks establish themselves in Poland in order to 'mop up' the considerable amount of dollars in private hands. Attracted by Western interest rates, this money would then be invested in the modernisation of Polish industry. The European Community is also looking afresh at its recently concluded bilateral economic agreements with Central and Eastern European countries to see how they can be gradually integrated into the Western European economy. Thus, all in all, there is no lack of ideas and specific initiatives for the mid-term goals of enhancing market forces in Central and Eastern Europe and integrating their economies into an overall neo-liberal Western trading system. What is essential is that Western help be directed not so much at governments but at specific projects of proven commercial viability. President Bush's endorsement of private enterprise trusts in Poland and Hungary has, in this respect, been the trendsetter.

Vision of a future Europe

Yet over the long-term, say 20 to 30 years, the economic renaissance of Central and Eastern Europe and the establishment of a post-Communist order in this region will succeed only if West can offer East a convincing vision of a future Europe. The West has first to recognise that helping Central and Eastern Europe is more than a humanitarian gesture or a means of easing a Yalta-induced guilt complex. If reform does not succeed, the consequences for the West will be far more catastrophic than the period of Cold War and painful division of the past half century. This did after all procure a relative stability at the price of injustice. We are moving paradoxically from a period of high tension, but also high stability, to a period of lower tension but also lower stability. Exacerbated by economic hardship, long-standing nationalist antagonisms have returned to the scene. We face the interesting prospect of three dimensions of tension: West versus West (Greece and Turkey); East versus "West" (Bulgaria versus Turkey following the forced exodus of over 300,000 ethnic Turks in the summer of 1989) and East versus East (Hungary, prior to the downfall of the Ceaucescu régime,

moved its army from the border with Austria to the borders with
Romania). As the walls come down between East and West, there is a
danger that they will go up between individual countries: physically, as
in the recent case of Romania building a fence to stop the clandestine
emigration of its Transylvanian Hungarian-speaking minority, or
psychologically, as in Polish anxieties over its post-war frontiers with
Germany. Already the troubles are making themselves felt. Slovenia
wishes to break away from Yugoslavia, the Baltic states are clamouring
for independence. Moldavians wish to be reunited with Romania. The
Soviet Union is increasingly paralysed by nationalist unrest, sometimes
directed against Moscow, sometimes appealing to Moscow for *'le juste
arbitrage'*. The side effects of these events have not been long in coming:
a million Poles have arrived in the Federal Republic, the United States
having encouraged the emigration of Jews from the Soviet Union now
finds itself having to place quota restrictions on the number it can
accept, and French farmers complain about potatoes arriving from
Central and Eastern Europe, along with Hungarian *'foie gras'* and Polish
pork. The approximately half a million Eastern German and other ethnic
Germans arriving in 1989 in the Federal Republic have put the housing
market and social security system under tremendous strain. Their
presence partly explains the rise of new right-wing parties.

The West does not wish to replace communism with the pre-war
authoritarian and confessional nationalisms that dominated Central and
Eastern Europe. We would not be able to insulate ourselves from the
spillover effects from prolonged unrest in this region. Along with
refugees would certainly come terrorism. The lesson of the Middle East
is that extremists would both seek Western support and also make the
West the scapegoat for all its frustrations. The numbers of Serbs,
Kurds, Armenians or Balts living in the Europe of the year 2000 could
make terrorism a veritable scourge for a privileged and inward-looking
European Community. Consequently, the Alliance nations must offer
Central and Eastern European reformers a concrete perspective of
association which they can use to contain popular impatience and
economic frustrations and combat also elementary nationalism, whether
from the newly-liberated, anti-semitic right or the old-guard unrecon-
structed Communists. It is at this level that Western thinking is still
in need of a clear definition. Both Western and Soviet leaders have been

unable to go beyond vague metaphors such as a 'Common European Home' or 'beyond containment'. Indeed it is essential that the Alliance be able to offer Europe Home, a term first coined by Brezhnev in the seventies. Despite its alluring overtones, it is still an idea in search of a precise definition. In his speech to the Council of Europe in Strasbourg in July 1989, Mr Gorbachev said that overcoming the division of Europe did not mean overcoming socialism. He has since warned the West against writing off socialism or trying to export capitalism to Central and Eastern Europe. His calls for non-interference imply that, on his side, no Soviet troops will put an end to change in Central and Eastern Europe but, on our side, we should not attempt to impose our values or system. With each new Gorbachev speech supplying an additional element, the Common European Home is emerging as a conception of a continent vastly more interdependent, stable and friendly than in the past, but still divided into two classical 19th century spheres of influence, with the interests and self-determination of the smaller countries sacrificed to the interests of the large. Gorbachev would seem to believe that Central and Eastern Europe can be stabilised around a third force concept combining market practice and socialist ideology, something that Mr Krenz during his short tenure in GDR called at 'market economy centrally planned system'!

The Alliance has little to gain from such a *status quo* plus arrangement, even assuming that the current momentum of change makes it a realistic objective. The Alliance's vision of Europe in the year 2000 was clearly set out in the Political Declaration issued at the May 1989 NATO Summit:

- a Europe of self-determination and individual freedom;
- a Europe where military force is no longer at a level where it can threaten other nations or maintain unjust political settlements; defensively structured military forces can be used only to preserve national sovereignty;
- a Europe where confrontation and ideological animosity is replaced by cooperation and peaceful competition;
- a new global environment founded on respect for individual rights, where all nations combine in a common endeavour to reduce world tensions, settle disputes, combat poverty and search for solutions to issues of universal concern, such as the environment, on which our common fate increasingly depends;

• an ever stronger Western community of shared values based on two equal pillars, European and North American.

These principles represent the essential foundation stone of the new Europe; but the European Home cannot be edified without a concrete political architecture. The acceleration of events following the May 1989 NATO Summit has issued the Western Allies with three urgent challenges that have reinforced the need for a more substantive architectural blueprint.

Shaping a new Political and Economic strategy

First, it is now clear that Central and Eastern Europe will not be a two-tier political system with some countries democratic and reformist and others remaining hardline Communist states impervious to change. The Alliance no longer has the luxury of dealing at leisure with Hungary and Poland, and then worrying about the GDR and Czechoslovakia years later. All the Central and Eastern European countries, with the exception of Albania, are now changing and Yugoslavia is disintegrating. So the Alliance now needs a political and economic strategy for the whole of Central and Eastern Europe, but one which is calibrated according to the status of reform and particular circumstances in each state.

Germany

Second, the issue of German unification has surged forward much more rapidly than anyone, East or West, had anticipated. It used to be believed that German unity would come at the end of a process of European unification, the *pièce de résistance* in an overall East–West settlement that had already been in operation for several years. The German question is now proceeding faster than the East–West question. It is not the Federal government but the population of the German Democratic Republic which is driving the process. With the Berlin Wall breached and the inter-German border open, the German population is already *de facto* reunited, and the call for unification, almost non-existent at the beginning of the protest movement in the GDR, is now growing. Some believe that a democratic and prosperous GDR will have more viability as a separate state, and that with open borders and economic exchanges, Germans will be less interested in a unification that was perceived initially as the way to procure these advantages. This was a view, however, that might well have been shared by Mr Modrow, former Prime Minister of the GDR, and the intellectuals and academics in the New Forum movement but manifestly not by ordinary GDR citizens who proved in the recent election that they want to enjoy the lifestyle of the Federal Republic. Only unification will offer this within an acceptable time-frame. Bonn will give economic assistance to a re-forming GDR as Chancellor Kohl has made clear. But this is a fraction of the investment Bonn will make in a Prussia and Saxony fully united with the Federal Republic. The Frankfurt-based Bundesbank, for instance, has estimated that providing the basic economic communications infrastructure (extension of the autobahn and rail systems) would cost DM 330 billion in the first five years. Moreover, the GDR united with the Federal Republic (FRG) will enjoy all the benefits of the 1993 Internal Market and full EC membership. Failing unification, there is a danger that industry in the FRG will see only the possibility of cheap labour in Leipzig or Dresden. Volkswagen, for instance, already produces car engines in East Germany and Zeiss optical instruments. Thus, it seems safe to bet that proximity, for the citizens of the GDR at least, will intensify rather than weaken the desire for German unity within a single state. Chancellor Kohl, in the 10-point plan he recently unveiled to the Bundestag, is probably right in thinking that confederation and federation are but near term stages on the road to this goal. Some Bundestag MPs have told the government not to bother to repair the Bundestag building in Bonn as it will not be needed for much longer. Other governments have deferred decisions concerning the maintenance of their Bonn embassies. At all events, German reunification instead of being a by-product of the new European architecture has become the key to everything else. It has become impossible to discuss the future rôle of NATO and the Warsaw Pact or the new European security system, before knowing the future shape of Germany.

Soviet policy

Third, the Alliance is having to come to terms with an increasingly reactive and not always coherent Soviet policy towards Europe. Since Mr Gorbachev came to power in March 1985, Alliance observers have been wondering where the new outer perimeters of the Brezhnev Doctrine lay: they were even expecting the next instance of dramatic change to provoke the long-awaited Soviet response as the threshold of tolerance was finally crossed. Now, however, we have to contend with Gennady Gerasimov's 'Sinatra Doctrine' according to which every state can 'do it its own way'. Perhaps there is no outer limit of tolerance at all. Another Soviet official has said that 'everything is possible in Eastern Europe provided it does not violate the laws of physics'. Like the declining imperial powers of the past, the Soviet Union may have lost the will to rule, its power reduced to bluff and, as such, only effective as long as the peoples of Central and Eastern Europe are not prepared to challenge it — but quickly revealed as hollow once they do. Yet on the other hand, the Soviet leadership warns against 'challenging the realities of World War Two', rejects German unification except on the condition of neutrality and denounces the imposition of capitalism. There is even interference after a fashion when we consider that Gorbachev's visit to East Berlin in October 1989 was instrumental in the removal of Honecker and that his successor, Mr Krenz, suddenly discovered his reformist credentials on his trip to Moscow soon thereafter. It is also clear that Romania's military leadership concerted at length with Moscow before rising against Ceaucescu. Of course, Gorbachev has not just passively accepted change in Central and Western Europe; he has provoked it. The old Warsaw Treaty Organisation leaders were only instruments of Soviet power. Once Gorbachev had withdrawn legitimacy from them, the aura of power collapsed and with it in a matter of days power itself.

Yet Soviet thinking on Central and Eastern Europe is highly ambiguous. Mr Shevardnadze calls for the dissolution of the two alliances, implying there is no structural difference between them and that together they pose an obstacle to change in Europe. Yet both Shevardnadze and Gorbachev tell Western leaders first in private and then publicly that they see the alliances as a vital element of stability and wish to preserve them — even to the extent of making the WTO into an Eastern version of NATO. Much of Gorbachev's early foreign policy pursued the old Soviet objective of driving the United States out of Europe; now he seems to welcome a continuing American presence. A similar change can be perceived in the Soviet campaign against American short-range nuclear missiles in Europe. Now Soviet experts acknowledge that a cooperatively structured minimal nuclear force on both sides in Europe could be a key factor in upholding military stability. One problem for Western analysts is that the Soviet policy-making establishment has now become as diffuse and unfathomable as that in the United States. *Glasnost* has seen a veritable Soviet invasion of officials, politicians and *institutniki* on to the Western conference and lecture-tour circuit. It is thus becoming difficult to know who speaks with authority for the Kremlin. A recent example was the interview given on American television by two Soviet commentators in which they said the Soviet Union would tolerate a Hungarian departure from the WTO. The following day their views were firmly rebuffed — albeit indirectly — by Mr Gerasimov. Was this a deliberate ploy to confuse the West, or evidence of disarray in senior Soviet circles? Is it simply a question of preparing for Soviet policy changes or testing the waters to glimpse the Western reaction? At all events, it has become essential for the Alliance to know far more of Soviet thinking on the future of Europe. Ambivalence must be resolved, and it indeed may be easier for the Kremlin to define its own thinking if it has a better grasp of Western ambitions in this field. The flurry of high-level East–West meetings in the final weeks of 1989 (Malta summit, Gorbachev's trip to Italy, Mulroney and Mitterrand's visits to Moscow) amply underline how both sides are aware of such a need for clarification, and a reasonably conciliatory approach — symbolised, perhaps, by the tele-vision image of a relaxed Soviet Foreign Minister paying a call on NATO's Secretary General Manfred Wörner on 19 December 1989.

Concentric circles

The Western architecture for Europe has still, however, to be defined. On his visit to Copenhagen, President Mitterrand spoke to journalists of the need to 're-invent Europe'. Most ideas have come in this respect from academics. Perhaps the most interesting is the concept formulated by Norbert Prill and Michael Mertes for a Europe made up of four concentric circles. In the centre would be a United States of Europe, made up of the original six EC members plus others, such as Spain who were prepared to accept a maximum of integration. The second circle would be composed of a European Federation including the remainder of the 12, plus perhaps the current EC candidates such as Austria or Turkey. The third circle would bring in the EFTA countries plus the newly-democratising nations of Central and Eastern Europe. Finally, the outer circle would comprise the 35 CSCE states, including the United States and Canada in the West and the Soviet Union in the East. Some have gone further and made the CSCE into a mini United Nations for Europe, with a peace-keeping rôle and perhaps a blue-beret force of its own to implement it. This outer layer could certainly operate as a sort of pan-European Council of Europe, handling human rights and cultural contacts as both a follow-up to, and extension of, the Helsinki process. The advantage of such an arrangement is that it would allow the European Community to balance two essential goals: to further deepen the cooperation among its members while extending a hand towards the newly emerging democracies in the East. Rather than attempt to settle on a fixed mould now for our concept of a future European architecture, we would no doubt be better served by this more flexible form of East–West cooperation and association, allowing states to move from the outer to the inner circles if and when they are ready. Europe, after all, needs a dynamic and not a static concept.

Despite the current wave of reform in Central and Eastern Europe, the Alliance, which has always coordinated Western policy towards the Conference on Security and Cooperation in Europe, must remain vigilant to ensure that the new as well as the old governments live up to their commitments in the framework of the CSCE — particularly the provisions on human rights and free movement of peoples and ideas first enshrined in the Helsinki Final Act, and subsequently tightened in the Vienna Concluding Document of December 1988. The various sub-groupings of the CSCE are hard at work on the implementation in practice of solemn commitments that all 35 participating nations have subscribed to. They cover such rudimentaries of daily democratic life as the free movement of journalists, bans on censorship, independent trade unions, freedom of religious education, rights of ethnic minorities, access to information, non-jamming of radio broadcasts, the granting of visas, freedom of emigration and unimpeded marriages between citizens of any countries.

Since the Vienna Follow-Up Conference of the CSCE, the West has obtained the right to comment directly on human rights abuses in the WTO countries, and to require a response. This new concession was used to pressure Romania (first by withdrawing EC ambassadors and then at the recent London conference on information, for instance) and the GDR and Czechoslovakia even before the current political changes began. An encouraging new development is that East now criticises East on human rights issues. Hungarians, for instance, have spoken out vociferously regarding the 'systemisation' policy in Ceaucescu's Romania which sought to uproot villages previously inhabited by the Magyar minority. Many have fled to Hungary. The Soviets and Hungarians have also abstained rather than support Romania in voting in the United Nations Commission on Human Rights in Geneva.

Yet despite these encouraging developments, genuinely free elections and the formal separations of the executive juridical and legislative branches of governments are not yet *faits accomplis*. The Soviet Union has still to change its legal code to make freedoms an inalienable right of citizens, backed up by independent institutions and not a favour granted at the discretion of governments, and other Central and Eastern European governments have yet to take convincing and lasting steps in this direction.

The CSCE process can also be used to build more bridges across the East–West divide. At their meeting in Brussels on 14–15 December 1989, NATO Foreign Ministers agreed that the CSCE process should be given a new impetus, particularly in reactivating the somewhat dormant Basket 2 of the Helsinki Final Act on technical, scientific and economic exchange between East and West. They also proposed to give CSCE more responsibility for East–West environmental issues. CSCE has been in the past a matter of government to government negotiation, but now it should also give rise to specific permanent bodies working on concrete cultural programmes.

The introduction of fully civic societies in Central and Eastern Europe is not merely a matter of recognised universal rights. It also requires the experience of practice and habit. The Soviet Union had a democratic constitution for years without ever becoming a democracy; Britain with no written constitution has been a democracy since 1689. Thus, while pressuring Eastern governments to make the necessary institutional and legal adaptations, the NATO Allies should look to direct people-to-people contacts to give Eastern citizens the tools to handle complex multi-party, pluralistic and market societies. Fostering democratic institutions and parliamentary exchanges is, of course, an idea in which the Council of Europe is particularly active. Up to now, it reserved membership to the parliamentary democracies of Western, Northern and Southern Europe. Yet thanks to their ongoing process of democratisation, Poland, Hungary, the Soviet Union and Yugoslavia were granted observer status. Once they have held free elections, guaranteeing human rights and the rule of law, all the nations of Central and Eastern Europe can join the Council of Europe as full members. They can then apply all the provisions of the European Court of Human Rights. In signing the numerous conventions of the Council of Europe, the newly emerging democracies of Central and Eastern Europe would join a network of cooperation encompassing in the future all the European nations in fields such as culture, transport, youth exchanges and the environment. The parliamentary assembly of the Council of Europe should transform itself into a parliamentary forum for the whole of Europe.

Yet while this new democratic order in Europe is being constructed, the member governments of NATO could take, individually and collectively, a number of initiatives both to speed up and strengthen the process of democratisation:

- inviting freely-elected Eastern parliamentarians to observe Western parliaments or the European Parliament in Strasbourg and participate in joint seminars with Western parliamentarians; the North Atlantic Assembly, NATO's parliamentarians' body, has made a useful start in this field by organising delegations to the Soviet Union, Hungary, Poland, and Czechoslovakia, and, recently, also an East–West parliamentarians' seminar in Bonn and a visit to NATO Headquarters in Brussels by a delegation from the Supreme Soviet;
- promoting exchanges of teachers and broadcasters;
- giving help to the new independent trade unions to organise;
- assisting the new political parties or opposition groupings to make their mark in election campaigns by helping with such

things as opinion sampling techniques, canvassing and electioneering methods and effective use of media;

- opening up Western universities to Eastern postgraduates, particularly in the fields of business, finance, marketing and banking or political science. (NATO is now offering several scholarships to citizens of the member states of the WTO for the study of democratic institutions — an embryonic programme in its present form, but one which could become the catalyst for a much more ambitious scheme in the future.)
- organising visitor programmes to enable successor generation Central and Eastern European leaders to tour government institutions and political organisations (such as parties, pressure groups and trade unions) in the West and to develop a permanent dialogue with them;
- stepping up Western information and cultural programmes in Central and Eastern Europe through local embassies and through increased support for bodies such as the British Council, Alliance Francaise and the Goethe Institut;
- increasing broadcasting output to Eastern Europe over BBC World Service, Deutsche Welle, Radio France Internationale, Voice of America, Radio Liberty and Free Europe. Western governments should also standardise cable transmission systems to enable the citizens of Eastern Europe to receive Western TV broadcasts — a facility enjoyed to date only by the citizens of the GDR (who receive FRG television) and the Estonians (who receive Finnish TV). The handling of the introduction of high definition television will be a key test of Western ability to create a single European communications network.

These ideas for a Europe of concentric circles or for a reinforced rôle for the CSCE are naturally only reference points in a debate. Yet the concentric circles idea has the advantage of balancing the requirement of self-determination with the requirement of order and structure across Europe. By playing down the significance of the nation state, it can help relieve the existing economic faultlines in Europe while allowing a return to the regional sub-groupings of cooperation of an earlier age. Examples of this are the Balkan conference, bringing together neutral Albania and Yugoslavia, NATO members Greece and Turkey and Warsaw Pact

Bulgaria, or the Quadrilateral Group of Austria, Italy, Yugoslavia and Hungary. At all events this concept highlights the need for the Alliance to describe the building blocks as well as the skeletal architecture of the future Europe. So far the debate has been somewhat transfixed by the Thatcher–Delors dispute over the future of European Community integration. On the one hand are the 'wideners' who point to the need for the Community now to embrace the reformist states of Central and Eastern Europe to secure their fledgeling democracies. On the other hand, we have the 'deepeners' who fear the consequences of a further 'Mediterraneanisation' of the Community if the addition of new, Central and Eastern European members is not offset by the membership of more rich, northern countries such as Sweden, Norway or Finland. The 'deepeners' believe that a united Europe of 12 with a single currency and enhanced institutional structures will have more economic and political cohesion to deal with Central and Eastern Europe's problems. Moreover, they worry that if the 1993 momentum is lost now, it cannot be regained later rather as one switches a tap off and on. They argue too that a Europe moving rapidly in its inner core will exercise centripetal pressures on Central and Eastern Europe, drawing it irresistibly into the central EC orbit. So far the deepeners appear to be winning over the wideners, particularly in the wake of the Strasbourg summit which moved firmly ahead on monetary union, but Mrs Thatcher is surely also right when she argues that the Community must offer Central and Eastern Europe a political perspective now. Integration must not become a byword for exclusivity. Reassurances will also be needed in other directions, for Turkey for example, hovering at the frontiers of the EC but so far denied admission because of alleged democratic or economic immaturity. If such is the reward for 40 years as a faithful member of the Alliance, the Turks might be forgiven for looking elsewhere for friends not necessarily of the West's choosing. So Europeans will need a certain acrobatic finesse in catering to all these requirements. Offering Central and Eastern European countries that pass certain basic tests of democracy and reformist sincerity associate membership under Article 231 of the Treaty of Rome has been strongly advocated by the Trilateral Commission. We can envisage also Eastern European involvement in EFTA as a temporary measure, particularly as the EC is currently negotiating closer cooperation with the EFTA countries.

The scope of these challenges and the nature of the Western reaction thus far enables us to identify three cardinal 'facts of life' for Alliance politics that are beginning to have important policy consequences for its future rôle.

In the first place, it is now clear that the central political and economic rôle in assisting the process of change in Central and Eastern Europe will be European rather than American. The facts of economic life are severe. Mr Bush originally asked for less than US $500 million for Polish and Hungarian reconstruction assistance. The US Congress has put the total up to US $900 million. But the Federal Republic alone has already approved loans to Hungary of more than US $300 million to be repaid in Polish currency. US $12 billion have been granted in different forms to Hungary and Poland alone, nine-tenths of this funding coming from Western Europe. Even neutral Switzerland is giving Poland credits with which to buy Hungarian beef. This is not to imply that the American economic rôle is insignificant; for instance the United States recently announced it is giving Poland US $25 million to improve the quality of air and water in the Krakow district. Yet it is clear that the Americans have been impressed by European confidence in a five per cent increase in Community GDP that economists predict will result from the 1993 Internal Market. It expects Western Europe to take the major rôle. President Bush has offered the Community 'leadership in partnership' — a far cry from 1975 when Henry Kissinger launched his 'Year of Europe' on the assumption that the United States has global and the Europeans only regional interests. At the same time, however, the Europeans cannot afford the illusion that they can manage historic transition without North American involvement. Transatlantic relations will only be complicated by American fears that Western European business is using its aid to corner markets in Central and Eastern Europe, thereby resurrecting the spectre of 'Fortress Europe' on a pan-European scale. Equally the United States will continue to take a close interest in Poland, with Chicago the world's second largest Polish city. And it will also be more involved than Western Europe in stabilising the overall East–West strategic balance, particularly in the fields of strategic nuclear weapons, regional conflicts and East–West cooperation in the United Nations.

Political consequences for NATO

Hence the crucial rôle of NATO in the next decade. To the extent that Washington wants to play a rôle in Europe, NATO is the best way whereby such influence can be channelled. It is, after all, the only Western policy-making institution that brings the United States and Canada together with Western Europeans. Neither the one side nor the other has by itself the political weight to stamp its exclusive mark on events. Transatlantic solidarity will be as essential for managing change tomorrow as it was for preserving stability yesterday. While Washington is pleased that Western Europe is showing signs of finally assuming its political responsibilities, some Americans will adjust badly to this new form of burden-sharing in which the United States can no longer make all good things happen, like the ass in Aesop's fable who said that he prayed every morning and the sun came up. The Bush Administration, however, is well geared to handle a more modest and realistic view of America's possibilities. It will be up to Europeans to play their full part in both Central and Eastern European and in global responsibilities. The view of some European academics that it is time to set up structures for a global division of labour may be damaging. Certainly the American rôle in Europe will be primarily a security one; the Community's rôle economic and environmental. But America must not be left with the impression that Europeans intend to shirk their military responsibilities, and that they wish to confine the United States to the 'unpleasant' military tasks while they attribute to themselves the 'pleasant' economic and cultural ones.

Another policy consequence for NATO is that the European divide will no longer be on the Elbe, but between 'Central' Eastern Europe and 'Eastern' Eastern Europe. As four nations, Hungary, Poland, the GDR and Czechoslovakia, move closer to the West, the others, the Soviet Union, Bulgaria and Romania, will lag behind. This is not because the latter group have not embraced change but because of severe economic problems and ethnic divergences that will retard the reform process. Increasingly, Western experts differentiate between the first category — where they are optimistic that Western aid can be decisive — and the second category — where they feel less certain of the future. For one thing, Soviet pride forbids, beyond immediate relief operations, the acceptance of 'aid' as such. Foreign Minister Shevardnadze, in a speech in the summer of 1989 to the New York Council of Foreign Relations, said that his country was looking for cooperation and not charity. Seeing history as the revolving wheel of fortune, he reminded his audience of the 1930s when two thousand Americans applied to emigrate to the Soviet Union to escape the hardship of the Great Depression. The American Secretary of State, James Baker, has suggested that the Soviet Union can best be helped by the creation of a peaceful international environment that will least divert Mr Gorbachev's attention away from the domestic agenda. This can be achieved through arms control treaties that will allow Soviet defence industries to be converted to civilian purposes, and a large proportion of the defence budget (officially given at 77 billion roubles) to be invested in consumer and capital goods. From an American perspective, it will 'lock the Soviets in' to a complex web of agreements and limitations that will make it more difficult and expensive for them to resort once more to Cold War diplomacy, should ever *glasnost* and *perestroika* fail.

Other ways of manifesting cooperation are to ease restrictions on technology exports, and to help the Soviet Union begin its integration into the world economy through membership of GATT, the IMF and the World Bank. President Bush's call on American business to invest in the Soviet Union at the Malta Summit is in such a benevolent but non-interventionist vein. If anything, it is an intellectual Marshall Plan for Mr Gorbachev that the United States advocates. It has sent high officials like Alan Greenspan, Chairman of the Federal Reserve Board, to Moscow to assess the situation and to determine what type of technical expertise is needed most. Helping to establish a reliable statistics system, previously missing entirely in the most centrally-planned of countries, such as the recent United States/Soviet-backed agreements on removing foreign troops from Angola and the restoration of independence to Namibia, is a further contribution to trust and stability. Yet the sheer dimension of the Soviet economy and its related problems, together with the much greater domestic uncertainties prevailing in that country, make it difficult for the West to go much further. We do not know towards which ultimate economic model Gorbachev is striving, no matter how much we admire his pragmatic skills. And it is possible that he does not know himself.

The third and final policy consequence for the Alliance is that the West must have an integrated strategy to manage change. The West cannot make its willingness to cooperate with Central and Eastern Europe an unconditional one, nor should it pretend that progress in one area (say economic interchange) can proceed merrily while the others are stagnant or even regressive. We must expect the Soviet Union and its former allies to meet us half-way and to prove that they too accept the conditions for fruitful cooperation. In particular, the allies will be looking for:

- continued Soviet willingness to allow the process of political and economic change towards democracy to proceed at its own speed in Central and Eastern Europe;
- conclusion at an early date of an agreement for conventional stability in Europe, particularly as regards the elimination of the Soviet Army's capacity for surprise attack and large-scale offensive operations;
- deepening Soviet commitment concerning resolution of disputes in the world's trouble spots;
- continuing Soviet engagement with the West on the new global threats to security; resulting for instance from the proliferation of nuclear, chemical and ballistic missile technologies in the Third World;
- acceptance on an agreed basis of concepts of stable nuclear deterrence resting on a minimal number of nuclear weapons in Europe.

This form of linkage is legitimate. Can the West, for instance, invest its money in the Soviet Union as long as that nation spends fifteen per cent of its GDP on weapons largely fielded against us? How can we persuade Western bankers to invest fresh resources in Hungary or Poland when countries such as the GDR and Czechoslovakia are either creditworthy or appear to have a brighter economic future? Mr Ceaucescu, while still in power in Romania, for instance, proved his outstanding creditworthiness by announcing at the beginning of May 1989 that his country had entirely paid back, and prematurely, its foreign debt. The unacceptable political price of such a policy was a decline in living standards of around 40 per cent in a single decade, food riots in Brasov and other towns, apartments that could not be heated above 50°F and light bulbs limited to 40 watts. So clearly, what suits Western bankers may not be entirely acceptable to Western foreign ministers. As long as economic aid is not linked to economic viability, and as long as the military situation in Europe shows an enormous Soviet conventional overhang — despite the spectacular changes — Western decisions *vis-à-vis* Europe will have to weigh a whole range of competing factors and arguments. Thus the final decisions will be eminently political. Only NATO has responsibility for East–West relations as a whole, and only NATO combines the major Western players. As long as an offer of cooperation has to be counter-balanced by the challenge of change, NATO is not only the best, but the only Western institution that can manage a global integrated strategy. NATO's integrated strategy is further justified because of the action–reaction character of *perestroika*. If Mr Gorbachev is to persuade his military and conservative colleagues to go down to minimal force levels, he will need to show evidence of broad East–West cooperation of immediate benefit to the Soviet economy. Thus a broadly-based Western political strategy of co-operation will be an essential part of achieving Western arms control objectives.

The conventions of international relations include respect for the legitimate defence of the long-term national interest. East–West economic contacts must be judged by that criterion no less than co-operation in the political sphere. As Article 2 of the Treaty of Washington of 1949 provides only for economic cooperation among the Allies, NATO will not therefore be responsible for specific aid pro-grammes directed at Central and Eastern Europe. These are already being handled by the 'Group of 24' whose actions in providing food aid and currency stabilisation credits are being coordinated by the European Community. The Group of 24 brings together all the Organisation for Economic Cooperation and Development (OECD) nations, and thus has the advantage of bringing the combined weight of nearly all the Western industrial nations to bear on the problems of Central and Eastern Europe. However, the Alliance, as a much tighter and more institutionalised form of Western cooperation than that pro-vided for in the Group of 24, does have a vital supervisory rôle to play in ensuring that economic as well as political measures promote irrever-sible change in a way that serves Western interests. Within the Alliance, each member country will act according to its own priorities, preferences and resources. Some will favour certain countries with which they have particular historic ties. Others will choose certain types of cooperation that they deem especially important or for which they feel particularly well-equipped. The rôle of NATO will be to provide the mechanism for coordinating all these national activities to ensure that they add up to an effective programme advancing Western interests.

At this time of unique historical opportunity, NATO must devise a sophisticated strategy to apply both challenge and reward simultaneously, in dialectical fashion. Although the challenges are things we would no doubt like Mr Gorbachev to do anyway, the rewards on offer have to be sufficiently substantial to function as incentives; even if they are in our long-term interest too. This will not be easy given the predilection of some to see the current situation in terms exclusively of opportunities, and others in terms exclusively of risks and dangers. Instead of moving closer together, the two camps tend all too frequently to frustrate each other in their mutually polarising positions. There will always be in the West a large group of Cassandra's advocates who will read the most negative interpretation into what the Soviets are doing. At a time of uncertainty and ambiguity, it will be difficult to prove that their worse case scenarios are either impossible or wrong. Yet perhaps the Alliance today needs more devil's advocates who are prepared to challenge the assumptions of their Cassandra counterparts with a more positive interpretation of events vindicating a more forward-looking Alliance policy.

Implications for the common defence

The Allies should not find it difficult to agree on the need to maintain a robust defence, despite budgetary limitations and perhaps continuing disagreements over the significance of individual military projects, such as the modernisation of short-range nuclear forces. There is always the possibility that *perestroika* will not succeed, and that a disturbed Soviet leadership will be tempted to resort to the military option as a way out of its internal problems. Certainly we do not need to be permanently suspicious of Soviet intentions, but we cannot proceed on the single assumption of Soviet goodwill. We want change but not to the extent of making our defence dependent upon change. Our preferred scenario must not be confused with the most unlikely scenario. NATO has to maintain a cautious guard, faced as it will be for many years to come by an over-armed power increasingly disturbed on the inside. Military intimidation may have failed in the past but the Soviet Union has frequently demonstrated a willingness to resort to it. The Alliance would be ill-advised to hand this option to the Soviet leadership on a plate by allowing its defences to rust away. To the extent that military intimidation becomes a risk-free option for the Soviets, they will be all the more tempted to use it. So defence will remain a prudent insurance policy against improbable but potentially disastrous contingencies. Kept at minimal nuclear and conventional levels, commensurate with effective deterrence, it can hardly be singled out by Mr Gorbachev as a brake on *détente* or an obstacle to meaningful East–West cooperation. So the Cassandra's advocates will have to give way on the Alliance's ambitious political strategy, while the devil's advocates must accept that as such a strategy means taking additional risks, it is only reasonable that those risks be underwritten by a firm insurance policy in the form of adequate security based on a realistic defence capability.

Clearly that defence capability does not need to be at the same level as today. The Alliance's goal is not minimum deterrence, as it is often claimed, but maximum deterrence with minimum weapons. It is true that weapons do not cause wars; they are the reflection of political tensions. But they are a factor that aggravates such tensions for if they can prevent wars, they can also facilitate them. The possession of overwhelming military force will frustrate genuine change in Europe by creating permanent doubts about political intentions, no matter how benign they appear on the surface. Thus, besides being increasingly an instrument of peaceful change, the Atlantic Alliance will be needed too as a framework of military stability on which that change can be permanently anchored. At the time of writing 50 per cent of all the divisions in the Atlantic to the Urals area are Soviet. Whereas only 11 per cent of the Europe-based NATO forces are American, 65 per cent of the WTO forces are Soviet. The military situation is changing, although less rapidly than the political situation. In the 1989 edition of its authoritative *Military Balance*, the International Institute for Strategic Studies stated that Mr Gorbachev's intended unilateral force cuts in Central and Eastern Europe (six divisions, 5,500 tanks plus airborne landing brigades) would, once carried out, remove the danger of a surprise Soviet attack. In recent months, the Pentagon has also acknowledged that for the first time since Gorbachev's arrival at the helm, Soviet spending and military production are slowing down, although not across the board. Yet the conventional imbalance remains and the Soviet Union retains, whatever its intentions, the capability for major offensive and terrain-seizing operations. The impressive timetables proposed by the Hungarians and the Czechs for the withdrawal of Soviet forces from their national territory will not in themselves alter this fact, although this development undoubtedly alters long held views on issues such as warning time. Against that, it is perhaps worth recalling the speed with which Soviet forces were put in place in 1956 and 1968. Their withdrawal is not irreversible. The reality of enduring military disparities must therefore be brought into line with hope for political cooperation. NATO's immediate objective must be to create a new East–West security system in which military forces are designed not to prevent change but cushion its turbulent side-effects.

There are two aspects to this objective. First to negotiate a régime of genuine and mutually-reinforcing military stability; and second to arrange an orderly reduction in force levels. The Alliance has established a firm conceptual leadership at the Vienna talks on Conventional Forces in Europe (CFE). An initial agreement in the course of 1990 is an agreed objective by both sides and is not beyond reach, given the impetus that both East and West have given to the talks — the Soviet Union in agreeing to — one might almost say embracing — Western suggestions for parity at certain residual levels in the main items of offensive equipment (tanks, artillery, armoured personnel carriers); the Allies agreeing to include aircraft, helicopters and United States forces in Europe, as the Soviets had long requested. Certainly, in such technically complex negotiations, which involve for the first time all the NATO and WTO members on an equal basis, there will be outstanding differences: for instance over definitions of equipment, counting rules, verification and so on. Yet these hitches are not insuperable obstacles. By the end of 1990 the Alliance, which has submitted a draft CFE treaty, will most likely have come to terms with a vastly different security environment: 60 per cent less Soviet forces and equipment in Central and Eastern Europe, and the prospect of 100,000 items of military equipment to be destroyed between both sides. Indeed Mr Genscher has proposed that both East and West agree, in addition to a CFE treaty, not to transfer such equipment at bargain prices to Third World countries in any shape or form. Ahead will lie CFE Mark 2, a new round of negotiations aiming for even larger reductions. The former Supreme Allied Commander, General Goodpaster, has spoken of a 50 per cent reduction; it will certainly be hard to settle for anything less than 25 per cent. Whereas NATO military commanders are confident that they can maintain the Alliance strategy of forward defence and flexible response with the 5 to 15 per cent reductions envisaged in CFE 1, that will become impossible with the much greater reductions of a CFE 2 that will not only thin out but eliminate entire NATO capabilities (such as divisions, air squadrons and troop to territory ratios).

Thus, while vigorously pursuing a CFE 1 agreement, it is imperative that the Alliance begin work now on a mid-term security concept to complement its mid-term political strategy. The following questions will need to be addressed:

First, what will be the definition of the security rôle of NATO when the traditional threat is no longer there? Countries that redirect their armed forces to cope with new or traditional regional threats will not want them unduly constrained by CFE. Since 1945, the threat to NATO has been moving constantly eastwards. Originally, that threat was from Soviet-supported Communist parties within Western Europe; then it was on the Central Front; by the end of the century it may be from instability — and Soviet forces — well inside the Soviet Union. With the reduced prospect of conflict in Central Europe, is there now an increased prospect of destabilising confrontation in Central and Eastern Europe which will require the NATO countries to elaborate effective new crisis management machinery? Perhaps it is time for NATO planners to remind themselves that the Washington Treaty was not directed only at the Soviet military threat but at all threats, including those of a non-military kind, to Allied security. Even with the Soviet Army out of Europe, we still live in a turbulent world and there are any number of threats around that demand a collective Alliance response.

Second, what will be the rôle of the United States in European defence? The United States Defence Secretary, Richard Cheney, has recently announced cutbacks that may extend to US $180 billion less

in projected spending over the next five years. Two Pentagon con-
sultants, Lawrence Korb and William Kauffmann, have advised that
the United States can provide for its security with only half its present
force levels. The solution to the Alliance burden-sharing problem would
seem to many to lie in burden-shedding: rather than the Europeans
going up to United States levels, the United States will come down to
European levels. The American rôle will be one of limited liability.
Certainly these American reductions will not be unilateral nor unco-
ordinated in the Alliance. President Bush expressly stated this at the
NATO Summit on 4 December 1989. Because of these pledges and
because of the receding Soviet threat, there is no reason why such reductions should cause alarm among Europeans. Moreover if economic
motives largely explain the cuts, there is no trace of 'declinism' in the
American posture. Paul Kennedy's thesis of imperial overstretch which
exercised such sway over the United States burden-sharing debate 12
months ago has now weakened. America is not cutting its losses. If it
does eventually decide to withdraw partially, it will be with its head
held high, for the sentiment in the Congress and among American public
opinion is that NATO is a job well done. Yet given the status of European forces and budget and manpower cuts on this side of the Atlantic
too, Western Europe alone will no more be able to defend itself
tomorrow against a smaller and more distant Red Army than it could
yesterday against the larger and closer one. American military involvement will remain crucial, and it will be up to the Europeans to tell
Washington what they consider its essential minimum to be. At the
moment, the figure of 195,000 United States troops in Central Europe
and a maximum of 30,000 elsewhere in Europe has been put forward
by the Bush Administration as the floor (minimum) and not the ceiling
(maximum). This figure is for negotiating purposes in the CFE talks
and would even, if accepted, leave the United States with more troops
outside national territory in Europe than the Soviet Union. Yet such
a disparity does not give the United States a strategic advantage due
to the fact that those troops will be 6,000 kilometres from their home-
land, the Soviet troops, on the other hand, barely 600 kilometres.
Congress, however, may still judge that, with a waning threat, 225,000
American troops in Europe is still too modest an overall reduction and
on balance not much cheaper to maintain. The status of the 195,000

in the central zone will also be affected by the shape of German unification whereby their presence at such a level could be considered erroneously as an 'occupying force' or control régime. Moreover the American presence in the Western half of the new Germany might be linked to the Soviet presence in the Eastern half, thus increasing the temptation for Moscow to make the withdrawal of its troops conditional on a United States withdrawal. Perhaps, as a result, future NATO military arrangements will take the form of a reversion to the original 1949 concept of NATO with Europeans providing the ground forces while Washington concerns itself essentially with nuclear cover, air forces and reinforcement capability. A residual United States presence in Europe at small levels would serve to signal American willingness to continue to act as a European power as well as symbolising the strategic military commitment. This should not, however, be left to the outcome of domestic debates and the vagaries of a Western structural disarmament that anticipates reductions before they have been negotiated.

Third, what will be the rôle of the WTO? Already Hungary is uneasy about a CFE 1 agreement because it fears that arms control treaty obligations will lock it irredeemably into membership of the WTO. References to a future Hungarian membership of NATO may not represent serious overtures but they speak volumes about the extent of Hungarian concerns. A way around this dilemma might be for the WTO to become more of a political grouping, settling disputes among its members. After all, Hungary and Romania will value its protection and Poland and Czechoslovakia will be wary of German unification outside a stable East–West security structure. Yet for the WTO to hold together, the Soviet Union must hold together — and peacefully. For if the Soviet Union can remain intact only through repression, its WTO allies will feel easy remaining within the Eastern Alliance. Like the Western Allies, the Soviet Union will have an interest in maintaining the proven frameworks of East–West stability; and in any case the WTO so depends on Soviet doctrine, equipment and training that it will be hard to disentangle completely.

Fourth, and finally, how will the CFE cuts be apportioned and how will NATO's future defence planning become fully compatible with arms control needs and obligations? There might, for instance, be a bid for entitlements; a country will not wish to be permanently excluded from a capability just because it happens not to have it at the time a CFE 1 treaty is signed (for instance Britain is procuring a new generation of helicopters). When it comes to eliminating equipment, the Alliance will face the complex task of apportioning the reductions in a way that is equitable and helps to relieve some of the long-standing disparities in burden-sharing. Yet the end result must be compatible with the maintenance of a robust defence; this will mean not only a rational localisation of the remaining equipment and forces but, more importantly, a posture that ensures that all the Allies continue to share the rôles, risks and responsibilities of the common defence. One problem will be to prevent the transfer of the military imbalance in the Central Region to the northern and southern flanks, particularly resulting in an increase in naval activities by both sides. For solidarity clearly demonstrated at the political level is as significant as hardware on the ground.

In the process, the Alliance will have to define what it conceives to be a 'defensive defence' — presumably a structure that not only gives maximum reassurance to the Soviet Union in peacetime but maximum reassurance to the Western Allies also should something go wrong. Certainly a 'defensive defence' will not necessarily be cheap: quality will have to compensate for quantity, more mobility for the additional space to be covered, more reserves and reinforcement forces for the fewer in-place stationed forces. Indeed, more transport capabilities may well be required to bring American and Canadian troops back to Europe at the onset of a crisis. Verification also will prove highly expensive. Hundreds of thousands of items of equipment and millions of troops will have to be checked — those that are to be destroyed, plus those that are allowed to remain. Twenty-three countries will be involved. The INF treaty, a comparatively simple verification job when one looks at a CFE agreement, already cost the US $50 million in verification in its first year of implementation. Thus it seems advisable for the NATO Allies to pool their resources and carry out verification collectively as Secretary of State Baker suggested in his Berlin speech on 12 December 1989. Otherwise the definition of 'defensive defence' may well end up being one NATO inspector in the East for every NATO soldier in the West!

Finally, CFE 1 and especially CFE 2 will lead to a massive shake-out of the West's defence industries. Companies are likely to merge or establish consortia to compete for the smaller number of contracts. Industry will need to produce new types of equipment that CFE does not constrain. On the other hand, governments will need to anticipate very high costs for such items as tanks, artillery and armoured personnel carriers due to smaller production runs and higher quality requirements. It will thus make even less sense than at present for NATO to produce four different types of main battle tank and five different types of attack helicopter. Such compression of the defence industrial base may in the long term make for efficiency, but in the short term the Alliance will have the problem of painful industrial conversion and resulting unemployment. This again is a task that the Allies can best address on a collective basis now, in order to have the most cost-effective division of labour throughout the Alliance. The way forward may well be for each country to specialise in a certain number of weapons systems and then sell them to its allies. Such an idea will be easier to formulate in theory than to translate into practice, given the industrial and high technology interests involved, but a planned Alliance-wide rationalisation is without doubt preferable in protecting national interests to simply 'leaving it to the market to sort it out'.

The lessons of history

The 19th century Greek poet, Costas Cavafis, once reflected on the people's need for an external threat as a stimulus for unity. 'What will happen to us,' he wrote, 'now that the Barbarians have gone?' For us, they were a kind of solution. Contrary to popular belief, however, the NATO Allies have always shared more than a common threat. The disappearance of a readily identifiable and obvious threat leaves NATO with an infinitely more complex and fragile political environment in Europe. As this commentary demonstrates, the old song rings true when it laments that 'there are more questions than answers'. Yet a modernised and dynamic Alliance is the only formula available to the West which can ensure conflict prevention in the short term and conflict resolution in the long term. Where would one look for stability and security if NATO were suddenly to disappear, whether by structural neglect or international treaty? Who would keep the United States and Canada committed to the destiny of a Europe in which they will continue to have a vital stake? Who would manage change by focussing the sum total of the West's political and economic resources on the challenges from the East? Without NATO, one can hazard a guess that the changes in Eastern Europe would seem far less exhilarating to Western public opinion. Indeed, if we were shrewd enough, without NATO, we would probably now be in an intensive negotiating process aimed at drawing up a North Atlantic Treaty designed to deal with the issues which we are bound to face in the 1990s. The Alliance provides essential re-assurance that we can maximise our opportunities while minimising our risks. The immense intellectual challenge of managing change while consciously shaping the future means that NATO as an organisation will of course undergo radical change. Following the May 1989 NATO Summit, it is already examining ways to reinforce its political tasks while winding down the military vestiges of the Cold War in an orderly fashion. The fact that in 1989, for the first time in its history, NATO held two summit meetings is testimony not only to the accelerating pace of events in Eastern Europe, but also to the accelerating swiftness of the Alliance's reaction. So it seems safe to predict that by the end of the century, NATO will not only be with us still, but that even more than in the past, it will be seen as the primary clearing house of Western policy-making — and this in a world of greater economic interdepen-dence, new global challenges from within our societies (drugs, pollution, crime) and from without (hunger, terrorism, regional conflicts) and in which the combined populations of Western Europe and North America will only make up six per cent of the world total. A vital task of NATO, given these challenges, will be to manage transatlantic relations and to prevent trade disputes over beef hormones, agricultural subsidies and the proportion of American soap operas in European television from deflecting attention from our common interest in staying together. Such considerations undoubtedly underlie President Bush's call for a 'new Atlanticism'.

History usually punishes two types of statesmen: those with too much vision and those with too little. The Alliance's task will be to combine the necessary prudence with the necessary imagination. But there will be the temptation of complacency. With Mr Gorbachev having a public relations field day by making or appearing to make unilateral concession after unilateral concession, and his former allies slipping their Eastern anchorage, the West may conclude that history has already delivered its verdict. Why intervene when things are running so strongly according to Western interests? Unfortunately, history is not made up of implacable historical laws which either work for or against specific causes. Things will only continue to go our way if we have the policies to shape events. Not least, the member countries of the Alliance must be active participants in the shaping of the wider, global security context which will be needed in the 21st century, in which countries like Japan, plus the emerging democracies of the Pacific and Latin America, will play an increasing role. The need for a suitable framework for discussion and cooperation with all the players involved is acute and will not go away. Some, who may be over-reacting, say that we must act today or by tomorrow the great opportunity will have disappeared. Yet it will certainly not last forever either. By the year 2000 the pattern of the future will have been decided, either for us or against us. After 40 years of its existence, the public still looks to NATO for solutions. Let it not disappoint them.

The Declaration of Paris
adopted by the
Atlantic Convention of
NATO Nations

19 January 1962

Foreword

THE Atlantic Convention of NATO Nations was an unprecedented meeting of more than ninety citizens appointed by the legislatures of the NATO countries. The Convention was held in the International Conference Centre in Paris, France, from January 8 to 20, 1962.

Though its citizen-delegates were officially appointed, they had only the authority to recommend, and they spoke and acted as individuals able to take a fresh and independent look at the problems of the Atlantic Community.

The first official call for such a Convention came from the NATO Parliamentarians' Conference in 1957. The need was reiterated by the Atlantic Congress in 1959, and repeated by the Parliamentarians in 1960. That year, too, the United States Congress enacted legislations setting up a United States Citizens Commission on NATO, and assigning it the task of bringing about and participating in the Convention.

The Convention was organised by an International Preparatory Committee of representatives of all NATO nations which met in London on October 26 and 27, 1961.

The purpose of the Convention was to explore and recommend ways by which greater cooperation and unity of purpose may be developed to the end that democratic freedom may be promoted by economic and political means. The result of its deliberations, which followed months of preparation, was the "Declaration of Paris" including a number of resolutions adopted unanimously by the Convention on January 19, 1962.

Atlantic Convention of NATO Nations

DECLARATION OF PARIS

We, the citizen delegates to the Atlantic Convention of NATO Nations, meeting in Paris, January 8–20, 1962, are convinced that our survival as free men, and the possibility of progress for all men, demand the creation of a true Atlantic Community within the next decade, and therefore submit this declaration of our convictions:

PREAMBLE

The Atlantic peoples have inherited a magnificent civilisation whose origins include the early achievements of the Near East, the classical beauty of Greece, the juridical sagacity of Rome, the spiritual power of our religious traditions and the humanism of the Renaissance. Its latest flowering, the discoveries of modern science, allows an extraordinary mastery of the forces of nature.

While our history has too many pages of tragedy and error, it has also evolved principles transcending the vicissitudes of history, such as the supremacy of law, respect for individual rights, social justice and the duty of generosity.

Thanks to that civilisation and to the common characteristics with which it stamps the development of the peoples participating in it, the nations of the West do in fact constitute a powerful cultural and moral community.

But the time has now come when the Atlantic countries must close their ranks, if they wish to guarantee their security against the Communist menace and ensure that their unlimited potentialities shall develop to the advantage of all men of goodwill.

A true Atlantic Community must extend to the political, military, economic, moral and cultural fields.[i] The evolution we contemplate will contribute to the diversity of achievements and aspirations which constitutes the cultural splendour and intellectual wealth of our peoples.

The Atlantic Convention, keeping this ideal constantly in view, recommends the following measures which, in its opinion, would foster the necessary cohesion of the West, would bring the final objective closer and should be adopted forthwith by the governments concerned.

SUMMARY OF RECOMMENDATIONS

1. To define the principles on which our common civilisation is based and to consult about ways of ensuring respect of these principles.

2. To create, as an indispensable feature of a true Atlantic Community, *a permanent High Council at the highest political level, to concert and plan, and in agreed cases to decide, policy on matters of concern to the Community as a whole.* Pending the establishment of the Council, the Convention recommends that the North Atlantic Council be strengthened through the delegation of additional responsibilities.

3. To develop the NATO Parliamentarians' Conference into a consultative assembly which would review the work of all Atlantic institutions and make recommendations to them.

4. To establish an Atlantic High Court of Justice, to decide specified legal controversies which may arise under the Treaties.

5. *To harmonise political, military and economic policy on matters affecting the Community as a whole.*

6. That the North Atlantic Council treat the development of an agreed NATO policy with respect to nuclear weapons as a matter of urgency.

7. That it welcome the development, progress and prospective expansion of European economic institutions, and the spirit of President

(i) Editor's italics.

Kennedy's statement that a trade partnership should be formed between the United States and the European Economic Community, *the basis of an Atlantic Economic Community, open to other nations of the Free World.*

8. That the Atlantic nations, acknowledging the right of every people to freedom, independence and pursuit of happiness, cooperate on a larger scale with the developing nations in their economic programmes, through direct and multilateral action: through the acceleration of investments; and especially through measures which would increase both the volume and value of their exports, including special tariff concessions for their exports.

9. *That the Atlantic Community take steps to help improve all their economies, so that the proportionate economic and social potential of all will be less unequal.*

10. That the Atlantic nations, noting the destruction of the national independence and the human rights of many peoples in Eastern and Central Europe, reaffirm their beliefs that the problem of these captive nations should be resolved in accordance with the principles of both *individual liberty and national self-determination.*

11. To create an *Atlantic Council for youth, education and culture* in order to draw up Atlantic plans for exchanges of young people, students and teachers and for the purposes of scientific and cultural collaboration.

12. That the NATO Governments promptly establish a special governmental commission to draw up plans within two years for the *creation of a true Atlantic Community, suitably organised to meet the political, military and economic challenge of this era.*

RESOLUTIONS

We, the delegates to the Atlantic Convention of NATO Nations, in meeting assembled, taking note of the recommendations of the NATO

Parliamentarians' Conference of 17 November, 1961 that an organised
Atlantic Community be created, have adopted the following documents:

PART I

POLITICAL AND ECONOMIC QUESTIONS

A. SPECIAL GOVERNMENTAL COMMISSION
TO PROPOSE ORGANISATIONAL CHANGES

Call upon the Governments of the NATO countries to draw up plans
within two years for the creation of an Atlantic Community suitably
organised to meet the political, military and economic challenges of this
era. To this end they should, within the earliest practicable period,
appoint members to a Special Governmental Commission on Atlantic
unity. The Commission should study the organisation of the Atlantic
Community, particularly in the light of the recommendations of this
Convention, and it should be instructed to propose such reforms and
simplifications of existing institutions, and such new institutions, as may
be required.

B. INSTITUTIONS

1. Recommend, as an indispensable feature of a true Atlantic Community, the creation, at the highest political level, of a Permanent High
Council, whose competence would extend to political, economic,
military and cultural matters. *Such a Council, assisted by a Secretariat,
would not only prepare and concert policies on current questions* and, in
defined cases, decide them by a weighted, qualified majority vote, *but
would also undertake long term planning and propose initiatives on matters
of concern to the Community.* All members of the Community would be
represented on the Council.

Whether this High Council be a new institution or a development
of the North Atlantic Council should be a matter of recommendation
by the Special Governmental Commission. In any event, however, pending the establishment of the Atlantic Community, the members of the
Convention *urgently request their governments to reinforce and develop the
North Atlantic Treaty Organisation as a political centre.* To this end, the
Convention recommends that the North Atlantic Council be strengthened through the delegation of additional jurisdiction. Where authority

for decision is delegated to the North Atlantic Council by governments, it should proceed by a weighted majority.

2. Propose that the NATO Parliamentarians' Conference be developed into a consultative Atlantic Assembly, to meet at stated intervals, or upon the call of its President or otherwise to receive reports regularly transmitted to it by the Secretaries General of other Atlantic bodies; to raise questions for and to consider, debate and review the work of all Atlantic institutions, and make recommendations to other Atlantic bodies and governments on questions of concern to the Atlantic Community. A permanent secretariat and an annual budget should be provided for the Atlantic Assembly to ensure continuity. In certain defined cases, recommendations should be by weighted majority vote. Members of the Atlantic Assembly would be selected by member governments in accordance with their constitutional procedure. They need not necessarily be Parliamentarians. The members thus chosen would have the power to elect a limited number of additional members of equal status.

3. Recommend the creation of a High Court of Justice, reserved to the Atlantic Community, in order to settle legal differences between members and between members and the organisations arising from the interpretation and application of treaties.

C. POLICIES

The institutions of the Atlantic Community should *harmonise those policies of its members affecting the interest of the Community as a whole, and contribute to the development of Community methods in planning, considering and executing such policies.*

1. A primary objective is the continuing expression through national and international action of an over-riding community of national interests in political and military policy. Closer and more effective action in this field should not await the growth of the Community institutions (see Paragraph B-2); the development of an agreed NATO policy with respect to nuclear weapons should, among other immediate problems,

be treated as a matter of urgency by the North Atlantic Council.

2. A second cardinal policy objective is to seize the opportunities for economic progress available through the creation and development of the Atlantic Community. The expanding European Economic Community is an economic advantage not only for its members, but for North America and the Free World as well. The Convention welcomes the spirit of President Kennedy's recent statement that a trade partnership should be formed between the United States and the European Economic Community. We hope that the negotiations envisaged by President Kennedy succeed in establishing a relationship which would constitute the nucleus of an *Atlantic Economic Community*, within the framework of Community institutions, open to all other qualified countries. Such a development would be of advantage to all countries, and particularly to those which participate directly in it. Among the fruits of this expanding Community would be its stimulus to competition, investment and more rapid growth in the mass markets appropriate to the modern technological age, with progressive reductions in tariffs and other barriers to trade.

3. Another important goal of the Atlantic nations is to *cooperate with those developing nations which wish to do so in their efforts to overcome the burden of poverty*, which may well be that of a falling per capita income in some countries. The Convention recommends that the Atlantic Community increase its already considerable participation in development programmes of this kind, through direct financial and technical measures; through increased shares in United Nations programmes, OECD programmes and other multilateral efforts; and above all through policies which favour commerce with and investments in the developing countries, such as the abolition of tariffs on tropical and primary products, and the reduction and, under agreed circumstances, even the eventual abolition of tariffs on their other products. The Convention also recommends the development of equitable and agreed programmes for the acceleration of investments, and for the protection of investors against political risks.

4. An important goal of the Atlantic Community's economic policies

should be to help *raise the standard of living and the level of economic activity of the different segments of the Atlantic Community*, so that the proportional economic and social potential of all members will be relatively less unequal.

5. In view of the hundreds of millions of hungry people living today, and the prospect that, if the present trends continue, there will be three thousand million more people added to the population in the next generation, the Convention recommends that the Atlantic Community should address itself forthwith to the population problem.

6. Since Soviet expansion has destroyed the effective national independence of many peoples in Eastern and Central Europe, denying to their individual members the free exercise of their religious rights and democratic liberties — with all the attendant injurious effects upon the general climate of European security and progress — the Convention affirms its recognition of the *inalienable rights of all nations to assume freely the responsibilities of self-determination and self-government*, and expresses its firm belief that the problem of the captive nations of Eastern and Central Europe should be resolved in accordance with the principles of both individual liberty and national self-determination.

7. As most governments of the Atlantic Community countries have accepted the obligatory clause of the statutes of the International Court of Justice at The Hague, the Convention recommends that all members of the Atlantic Community accept this obligatory clause.

PART II

MORAL AND CULTURAL QUESTIONS

A. The Atlantic Convention of NATO Nations *Declares* that the basic moral and spiritual principles upon which the lives and acts of the nations forming the Atlantic Community are based are as follows:

1. *The purpose of political and economic institutions is the protection and promotion of the rights, liberties and duties which enable every human being to fulfil his or her spiritual vocation;*

2. Liberty is inseparable from responsibility, which implies recognition of a moral law to which men, as individuals and in groups, are subject;

3. Liberty is inseparable from the duties of men towards one another, which implies the obligation to ensure that all men gradually attain physical and moral well-being;

4. Liberty is inseparable from tolerance, which recognises the right to free discussion of all opinions which are not in violation of the very principles of civilisation;

5. *There can be no freedom without variety*, the natural result of the different origins and varying achievements of different peoples in all fields. *But this variety should not entail disunity.* On the contrary, retaining the common factors, it should become the permanent force impelling the peoples of our Western civilisation to unite;

6. Freedom is inseparable from the spirit of objective truth, which must restore to words the exact meaning they have in the Free World.

And therefore *invites* members countries:

1. To defend and promote the values and principles of civilisation by means of education, publications, lectures, radio, the cinema and television;

2. To uphold in their conduct with all nations the ethics and values of Western civilisation and by their example to impress on others that discord and disunity result when they are not observed;

3. To defend these values and principles against intellectual and moral subversion within the Community;

4. To try to establish an atmosphere of mutual understanding between the members of the Atlantic Community, appreciating to the full

the riches of their diversity;

5. To demonstrate to all peoples that respect for these values and principles can alone make a technological civilisation an instrument for improving the physical and moral well-being of mankind;

RECONSTRUCTION OF THE ACROPOLIS

To decide that the Acropolis shall become the symbol of our culture and the shrine of our Alliance and to call upon governments to consider how this resolution might be given concrete form.

B. The Atlantic Convention of NATO Nations: *Considering* that a major obstacle to the formation of real European and Atlantic Communities is the difference in language and therefore in mentalities and ways of thinking: *Considering* that this language barrier is particularly prejudicial to the scientific cooperation upon which the Western potential depends:

Invites the Governments of NATO nations, and such other countries as may be inspired by the same ideal, *to convene an Atlantic Council consisting of Ministers of Education, Ministers for Scientific Affairs, cultural and educational authorities and representatives of universities and scientific research organisations*, with a view to:

1. Determining the comprehensive aims of an education likely to promote the ideals and purposes of the Atlantic Community, studying ways and means of implementing the principles laid down, and periodically reviewing the results achieved.

2. Organising:
   a bold Atlantic Plan for Youth and Education with the aim of furthering the study of languages and the widest possible exchange of students, teachers and youth leaders and of workers in industry and agriculture,
   a programme of scientific cooperation among the scientists and the scientific institutions of the countries of the Community,
   both of the above being financed by all participating nations.

Within the framework of the above recommendations, the Convention *draws the attention of governments* to the following points:

a. Alongside the study and use of foreign languages, it is essential that mutual understanding be developed between men with different ways of thinking from all parts of the Free World, including those of the emergent nations. This programme should in the first place benefit university students, as many as possible of whom should be enabled to spend at least one year of their course in a university or other advanced training establishment where teaching is in a language other than their own.

However, in the case of the most promising citizens of the emergent nations this programme should have a special priority, since their intellectual hunger must be satisfied at all costs.

Steps will have to be taken to ensure that such periods spent at foreign universities or other establishments do not prejudice the career of the student concerned but rather confer advantages upon him in the form of either a degree valid in his own country or a new type of degree specially created for the purpose of enabling him, for instance, to exercise his profession either in his own country or in that where he has completed one or more years of study, always providing that his knowledge of the two languages is sufficient.

b. It is to be hoped that, in the future, those who have pursued such a course of training, which would subsequently be supplemented by exchanges of civil servants between Atlantic nations, will be given priority in selection for posts as officials required to take part in international negotiations.

c. It should be made possible for teachers, and particularly university teachers, research workers and curators of museums and art galleries, either to be seconded periodically to equivalent foreign organisations, or to establish close contacts with them. Although it may not be immediately possible for all Atlantic Community countries, the introduction of the system of the 'sabbatical year' for teachers and research workers would be generally desirable.

d. In the field of scientific documentation and cooperation, it would be necessary to supplement existing organs by setting up a *Scientific Documentation Centre* responsible, among other things, for the translation and distribution of the principal articles, reports and other publications appearing throughout the world which have not yet been distributed by other agencies. The Convention considers this a most urgent matter.

e. The 'pairing-off' of universities and other advanced educational establishments of different languages within the Community should be encouraged and intensified.

f. The establishment and exchange of comparable statistics on education and research in the Atlantic Community countries should be assured.

C. The Atlantic Convention of NATO Nations recommends that these proposals be studied further by the Atlantic Institute in order to assist in the accomplishment of these tasks in cooperation with existing agencies, such as the Council for Cultural Cooperation of the Council of Europe, so as to avoid duplication of effort.

GENERAL RESOLUTION

The Atlantic Convention of NATO Nations requests its President to forward the foregoing Declaration and Resolutions to the NATO Council and to the NATO Parliamentarians' Conference at the earliest possible date, and that the delegates to this Convention report the same to their respective Governments or legislative authorities at their earliest convenience.

Atlantic Convention of NATO Nations

Chairman

HON. CHRISTIAN A. HERIER (U.S.A.)

Vice-Chairmen

GENERAL A. BELHOUART (France)
DR. MARTIN BLANK (German Federal Republic)
LORD CRATHORNE (U.K.)
SENATOR PIETRO MICARA (Italy)
Mr. PATRICK NICHOLSON (Canada)
M. PAUL VAN ZEELAND (Belgium)

Secretary General

MR. RICHARD J. WALLACE, JR (U.S.A.)

Members of the Convention

COUNT RABAN ADELMANN (German Fed. Rep.)
MR. DONALD AGGER (U.S.A.)
PROF. MAURICE ALLAIS (France)
MR. K. P. ANDRAS (Canada)
GENERAL P. BILLOTTE (France)
BARON BOEL (Belgium)
MR. UMBERTO BONALDI (Italy)
PROF. DR. LEO BRANDT (German Fed. Rep)
DR. MAX BRAUER (German Fed. Rep.)
THE HON. A. BUCHAN (U.K.)
HON. WILLIAM A. BURDEN (U.S.A.)
MR. JEAN CHAMANT (France)
MR. MICHELE CIFARELLI (Italy)
HON. WILLIAM L. CLAYTON (U.S.A.)
MR. ARTHUR CONTE (France)
MR. RAYMOND CORY (U.K.)
REVEREND PÈRE DANIELOU (France)
LORD DUNDONALD (U.K.)
MR. CHARLES W. ENGELHARD, JR (U.S.A.)
MR. GIUSEPPE ERMINI (Italy)
PROF. AHMET SÜKRÜ ESMER (Turkey)
MR. GEORGES J. FELDMAN (U.S.A.)
MR. MARCEL FISHBACH (Luxembourg)
MR. MORRIS FORGASH (U.S.A.)
DR. W. F. DE GAAY FORTMAN (Netherlands)
MR. GUNNAR GARBO (Norway)
MR. DONALD GILLIS (Canada)
MR. MOHEMET GÖNLÜBOL (Turkey)
MR. R. GOOLD-ADAMS (U.K.)
MR. G. J. H. DE GRAAFF (Netherlands)
MR. H. F. HALLGRIMSSON (Iceland)
MR. GEORGES HEREIL (France)
MR. HULPIAU (Belgium)
MR FRANCIS HUTCHINS (U.S.A.)
DR. EUGEN HUTH (German Fed. Rep.)
MRS. HERTA ILK (German Fed. Rep.)
MR. ERIC JOHNSTON (U.S.A.)
MR. DANIS KOPER (Turkey)
MR. OLE BJORN KRAFT (Denmark)
MR. WALDEMAR KRAFT (German Fed. Rep.)
MR. PIERRE LAZAREFF (France)
MR. IVAN MATTEO LOMBARDO (Italy)
MR. EINAR MAGNUSSON (Iceland)

MR. PER MARKUSSEN (Denmark)
MR. ARMANDO MARTINS (Portugal)
LT.-GEN. T. E. E. H. MATHON (Netherlands)
MR. JOHAN MELANDER (Norway)
MR. ORHAN MERSINLI (Turkey)
PROF. MARIO MONTANARI (Italy)
MR. HUGH MOORE (U.S.A.)
MR. NAESSENS (Belgium)
LORD OGMORE (U.K.)
MR. R. T. PAGET (U.K.)
MR. J. P. PALEWSKI (France)
MR. JOHN PALLETT (Canada)
PROF. UGO PAPI (Italy)
MR. RALPH D. PITMAN (U.S.A.)
PROF. G. PORTMANN (France)
MR. BEN REGAN (U.S.A.)
MR. STEPHEN B. ROMAN (Canada)
MR. ELMO ROPER (U.S.A.)
MR. I. SAMKALDEN (Netherlands)
MRS. EDITH S. SAMPSON (U.S.A.)
MR. JOHN SANNESS (Norway)
MR. FRIEDRICH SAROW (German Fed. Rep.)
MR. ADOLPH SCHMIDT (U.S.A.)
MR. OLIVER C. SCHROEDER (U.S.A.)
MARSHAL OF THE R.A.F SIR JOHN SLESSOR (U.K.)
MR. ALISTAIR STEWART (Canada)
MR. BURR S. SWEZEY (U.S.A.)
MR. H. E. THRASYVOULOS TSAKALOTOS (Greece)
MRS. LINA TSALDARIS (Greece)
MR. ATHOS VALSECCHI (Italy)
MR. GIUSEPPE VEDOVATO (Italy)
MR. PAUL VISSING (Denmark)
SENATOR W. M. WALL (Canada)
MR. GERHARD WALTHER (German Fed. Rep.)
MR. ALEXANDER WARDEN (U.S.A.)
SIR THOMAS WILLIAMSON (U.K.)
DR. FRIEDRICH WINIER (German Fed. Rep.)
MR. DOUGLAS WYNN (U.S.A.)
MR. AHMLI EMIN YALMAN (Turkey)
MR. YAZICI (Turkey)
SENATOR RAUL ZACCARI (Italy)

Treaty Establishing the European Defence Community

Signed at Paris, 27 May 1952

Historical Note on the European Defence Community (EDC)

At the instigation of the French Prime Minister, René Pleven, negotiations opened in Paris in February 1951 for the creation of a European Defence Community consisting of France, Italy, the Benelux countries and the Federal Republic of Germany. Guarantees were provided under the terms of a Protocol signed by the North Atlantic Treaty governments. Negotiations continued until May 1952 when the European Defence Community Treaty was signed. The United Kingdom did not see its future in the form of the European federation to which the EDC was expected to lead, and participated in the EDC negotiations only as an observer. However, it was made clear that the EDC came firmly within the framework of the North Atlantic Treaty and that countries such as Britain would consequently be directly concerned both through NATO and through additional multilateral arrangements. Against this background, the EDC represented an ambitious solution which came near to succeeding. The detailed EDC Treaty was signed by all six continental European member countries (France, Italy, Germany, Belgium, the Netherlands and Luxembourg), i.e. all the members of the embryonic European Coal and Steel Community established under the 1950 Schuman plan, forerunner of the Common Market.

The 1948 Communist coup in Czechoslovakia and the outbreak of the Korean war in 1950 served to heighten European and American apprehensions about Soviet expansionist policies and to bring home the need to mobilise the full resources of Western Europe to meet the threat. This meant that moves to organise the defence of Europe and arrangements to enable German armed forces to participate had to be accelerated. The proposed EDC was enthusiastically supported by the United States, and the process of parliamentary ratification, which was needed before the Treaty could be implemented, was completed by all countries except Italy and France. On 29 August 1954 the French National Assembly decided against ratification of the Treaty and the project had to be shelved.

The question of the future role of Germany in the defence of Western Europe was finally solved with the signature of the Paris Agreements of 23 October 1954, and in May 1955 the Federal Republic of Germany acceded to the North Atlantic Treaty.

Table of Contents

TREATY

PREAMBLE

PROTOCOLS

NOTES

1. This is an unofficial translation of the European Defence Community Treaty. It utilises both the text appearing in the US Senate publication 94118 (82d Congress, 2nd Session, Executive Q and R), referred to the Committee on Foreign Relations on 2 June, 1952, and the translation prepared by the NATO Secretariat and published as Document ISM(52)18 on 12 June, 1952, as well as the translation of Annex II to Article 107 agreed tripartitely in Bonn by the General Secretariat of the Allied High Commission in Germany.

   The present translation contains, however, certain revisions designed to ensure the greatest possible exactitude. The arrangement of the related Protocols follows the pattern of the official French text published by the French Foreign Office (undated). Amendments agreed upon subsequent to the publication of the Senate and NATO translations have also been included.

2. A total of 19 Protocols, common declarations and exchanges of letters were appended to the Treaty. Five of these are reproduced here (see Table of Contents). The others were as follows:

   - Military Protocol
   - Jurisdictional Protocol
   - Military Penal Law Protocol
   - Financial Protocol
   - Conditions of Remuneration and Pension Rights of the Civil and Military Personnel employed by the Community
   - Protocol Relative to the Status of European Defence Forces and the Tax and Commercial Régime of the EDC
   - Signature Protocols
   - Common Declaration by the Ministers of Foreign Affairs Concerning the Duration of the Treaty
   - Protocol Concerning the Interim Committee
   - Agreement Provided for in Article 107
   - Exchange of Letters between the Government of the Federal Republic of Germany and the Governments of the Co-Signatory States to the Treaty constituting the EDC concerning Article 107 of the Treaty
   - Appendix relating to the Control of Atomic Energy and to Civilian Aircraft

Treaty Establishing the European Defence Community

PREAMBLE

The President of the Federal Republic of Germany, His Majesty the King of the Belgians, the President of the French Republic, the President of the Italian Republic, Her Royal Highness the Grand Duchess of Luxembourg, Her Majesty the Queen of the Netherlands.

Resolved to contribute to the maintenance of peace, particularly by ensuring the defence of Western Europe against any aggression, in cooperation with the free nations, in the spirit of the United Nations Charter, and in close liaison with organisations having the same purpose;

Considering that as complete an integration as possible, compatible with military requirements, of the human and material elements gathered in their Defence Forces within a supranational European organisation is the most appropriate means of reaching this goal with all the necessary speed and efficiency;

Certain that such integration will result in the most rational and economic use of the resources of their countries, as a result, particularly, of the establishment of a common budget and of common armament programs;

Determined thereby to secure the expansion of their military forces without detriment to social progress;

Desirous to safeguard the spiritual and moral values which are the common heritage of their peoples, and convinced that within a common army constituted without discrimination among the participating States national patriotisms, far from being weakened, can only become consolidated and harmonised in a broader framework;

Conscious that they are thus taking a new and essential step on the road to the formation of a united Europe;

Have decided to create a European Defence Community and to this end have designated as plenipotentiaries :

The President of the Federal Republic of Germany, Dr. Konrad Adenauer, Chancellor, Minister of Foreign Affairs.

His Majesty the King of the Belgians.

Mr. Paul Van Zeeland, Minister of Foreign Affairs;

The President of the French Republic,

Mr. Robert Schuman, Minister of Foreign Affairs;

The President of the Italian Republic,

Mr. De Gasperi, Minister of Foreign Affairs;

Her Royal Highness the Grand Duchess of Luxembourg,

77

Mr. Bech, Minister of Foreign Affairs;
Her Majesty the Queen of the Netherlands,
Mr. Stikker, Minister of Foreign Affairs;
Who, after having exchanged their credentials and found them in good and due form, have agreed upon the provisions which follow.

Title I
Fundamental Principles

Chapter I
European Defence Community

Article 1
By the present Treaty the High Contracting Parties institute among themselves a European Defence Community, supranational in character including common institutions, common armed Forces and a common budget.

Article 2
1. The objectives of the Community are exclusively defensive.

2. Consequently, under the conditions provided for in the present Treaty, it shall ensure the security of the member States against any aggression by participating in Western Defence within the framework of the North Atlantic Treaty and by achieving the integration of the defence forces of the member States and the rational and economic utilisation of their resources.

3. Any armed aggression directed against any one of the member States in Europe or against the European Defence Forces shall be considered an attack directed against all of the member States.

The member States and the European Defence Forces shall furnish to the State or Forces thus attacked aid and assistance by all means, military and other, in their power.

Article 3
1. The Community shall employ the least burdensome and most efficient methods. It shall intervene only to the extent necessary for the fulfillment of its mission and with due respect to public liberties and fundamental rights of the individuals. It shall see to it that the individual interests of member States are taken into consideration to the full extent compatible with its own essential interests.

2. In order to enable the Community to reach its goals, the member States shall place at its disposal appropriate contributions determined under the provisions of Articles 87 and 94 hereinafter.

Article 4
The Community shall pursue its action in cooperation with the free nations and with any organisation whose goals are the same as those of the Community.

Article 5
The Community shall cooperate closely with the North Atlantic Treaty Organisation.

Article 6
The present Treaty does not involve any discrimination among the member States.

Article 7
The Community shall have a legal personality. In its international relations, the Community shall have the legal capacity necessary for the exercise of its functions and the attainment of its aims.

In each member State, the Community shall enjoy the widest juridical capacity granted to national legal entities; in particular, it shall be empowered to acquire and transfer real and personal property and to institute judicial proceedings.

The Community shall be represented by its various institutions, each acting within the framework of its capacity.

Article 8
1. The institutions of the Community shall be :
   — a Council of Ministers, hereinafter referred to as the Council.
   — a Common Assembly, hereinafter referred to as the Assembly.
   — a Commissariat of the Community, hereinafter referred to as the Commissariat.
   — a Court of Justice, hereinafter referred to as the Court.

2. Without prejudice to the provisions of Article 126 below, the organisation of the institutions as established by the present Treaty shall remain in effect until it is replaced by a new one, resulting from the establishment of a federal or confederal structure as provided in Article 38 hereinafter.

Chapter II
European Defence Forces

Article 9
The Armed Forces of the Community, hereinafter referred to as 'European Defence Forces', shall be composed of contingents placed at the disposal of the Community by the member States with a view to their fusion under the conditions provided for in the present Treaty.

No member State shall recruit or maintain national armed forces aside from those provided for in Article 10 hereinafter.

Article 10
1. The member States may recruit and maintain national armed forces intended for use in the non-European territories with respect to which they assume defence responsibilities, as well as units stationed in their own countries which are required for the maintenance of these forces and for their relief.

2. The member States may also recruit and maintain national armed forces required for international missions assumed by them in Berlin, in Austria or arising out of decisions of the United Nations. At the termination of these missions, these troops shall be either disbanded or placed at the disposal of the Community. Relief for these troops may be effected with the consent of the competent Supreme Commander responsible to the North Atlantic Treaty Organisation, by exchange with units composed of contingents belonging to the European Defence Forces and originating in the member States in question.

3. In each member State elements intended as a bodyguard for the Chief of State shall remain national.

4. The member States may dispose of national naval forces, on the one hand for the protection of non-European territories for which they assume defence responsibilities as mentioned in Paragraph 1 of this Article and for the protection of communications with and among such territories, and on the other hand to fulfill the obligations resulting from the assumption by them of international missions referred to in Paragraph 2 of this Article and as a result of agreements entered into within the framework of the North Atlantic Treaty prior to the entry into force of the present Treaty.

5. The total size of the national armed forces referred to in the present Article, including maintenance units, shall not be so large as to jeopardise the contribution of any member State to the European Defence Forces, as determined by agreement between the Governments of the member States.

The member States shall have the right to exchange individual personnel between the contingents placed by them at the disposal of the European Defence Forces and the forces which are not a part thereof, provided, however, that no reduction in the European Defence Forces occurs as a result.

Article 11

Police forces and forces of gendarmerie, intended exclusively for the maintenance of internal order, may be recruited and maintained by the member States.

The national character of these forces is not affected by the present Treaty.

The volume and nature of the said forces existing on the territories of member States shall be such as not to exceed the limitations of their mission.

Article 12

1. In case of disturbances or threats of disturbances on the territory of a member State in Europe, such part of the contingents supplied by such State to the European Defence Forces as is necessary to meet the situation shall, at its request, and upon notification to the Council, be placed at its disposal by the Commissariat.

The conditions under which these elements may be employed shall be determined by the regulations in force on the territory of the member State making the request.

2. In case of disaster or catastrophe requiring immediate aid, such elements of the European Defence Forces as may be in a position to be of use shall give their aid without regard to their national origins.

Article 13

In case of a serious emergency affecting a non-European territory for which a member State assumes responsibilities of defence, such part of the contingents supplied by such State to the European Defence Forces as is necessary to meet the emergency shall, on its request and with the agreement of the competent Supreme Commander responsible to the North Atlantic Treaty Organisation, be placed at its disposal by the Commissariat, upon notification to the Council. The contingents thus released shall cease to be subject to the authority of the Community until such time as they are once again placed at its disposal when they are no longer needed to meet the emergency.

The military, economic and financial implications of the withdrawal of contingents provided for in this Article shall, in each case, be examined and settled by the Commissariat with the concurrence of the Council given by a two-thirds majority vote.

Article 14

In case an international mission, to be fulfilled outside the territory defined in Paragraph 1, Article 120, is entrusted to a member State, such part of the contingents supplied by such State to the European Defence Forces as is necessary to fulfill the mission shall, on its request and with the agreement of the competent Supreme Commander responsible to the North Atlantic Treaty Organisation, be placed at its disposal by the Commissariat with the concurrence of the Council given by a two-thirds majority vote. The contingents thus released shall cease to be subject to the authority of the Community until such time as they are once again placed at its disposal when they are no longer needed for the fulfillment of the said mission.

In such a case, the provisions of Paragraph 2, Article 13, above, shall be applicable.

Article 15

1. The European Defence Forces shall be made up of personnel recruited by conscription and of career or volunteer, long-service personnel.

2. The European Defence Forces shall be integrated in accordance with the organic provisions of Articles 68, 69 and 70 hereinafter.

They shall wear a common uniform.

They shall be organised according to the types defined in the Military Protocol. Such organisation may be modified by unanimous decision of the Council.

3. The contingents intended to make up the units shall be provided by member States in accordance with a plan for their constitution to be determined by agreement among member Governments. This plan may be revised under the conditions set forth in Article 44 below.

Article 16

The internal defence of the territories of the member States against attacks of any nature having military ends and provoked or carried out by an external enemy shall be ensured by homogeneous formations of European status, which shall be specialised in each country in accordance with the particular defence mission required by its territory and whose use shall be decided upon by such authorities as are defined in Article 18 hereinafter.

Article 17

The protection of the civilian population shall be ensured by each of the member States.

Article 18

1. The competent Supreme Commander responsible to the North Atlantic Treaty Organisation shall, except as provided in Paragraph 3 of this Article, be empowered to ensure that the European Defence Forces are organised, equipped, trained and prepared for duty in a satisfactory manner.

As soon as they are ready for use, the European Defence Forces shall, except as provided in Paragraph 3 of this Article, be assigned to the competent Supreme Commander responsible to the North Atlantic Treaty Organisation, who shall exercise with respect to them the powers and responsibilities accruing to him under his terms of reference and shall specifically submit to the Community his needs as regards the articulation and deployment of these Forces; the corresponding plans shall be worked out in accordance with the provisions of Article 77 hereinafter.

The European Defence Forces shall receive technical directives from the appropriate bodies of the North Atlantic Treaty Organisation within the framework of the military competence of such bodies.

2. During wartime, the competent Supreme Commander responsible to the North Atlantic Treaty Organisation shall exercise with regard to the Forces provided for above the full powers and responsibilities of Supreme Commanders, such as are conferred upon him by his terms of reference.

3. In the case of units of the European Defence Forces assigned to internal defence and the protection of the sea approaches of the territories of member States, determination of the authorities to whom they shall be subordinate for Command purposes and employment shall depend either on conventions concluded within the framework of the North Atlantic Treaty or on agreements between the North Atlantic Treaty Organisation and the Community.

4. If the North Atlantic Treaty should cease to be in effect before the present Treaty, the member States shall, by agreement among themselves, decide upon the authority to which the command and employment of the European Defence Forces shall be entrusted.

Title II
Institutions of the Community

Chapter I
The Commissariat

Article 19

The Commissariat, with a view to carrying out the tasks assigned to it by virtue of the present Treaty, shall be vested with executive and supervisory powers as provided in the present Treaty.

Article 19 bis

The Commissariat shall assume its functions as of the appointment of its members.

Article 20

1. The Commissariat shall be composed of nine members appointed for six years and chosen for their general competence.

Only nationals of the member States may be members of the Commissariat. It may not include more than two members of the same nationality.

Members shall be eligible for reappointment. The number of members of the Commissariat may be reduced by unanimous decision of the Council.

2. In the discharge of their duties, the members of the Commissariat shall neither solicit nor accept instructions from any Government. They will abstain from any act incompatible with the supranational character of their functions.

Each member State agrees to respect this supranational character and not to seek to influence the members of the Commissariat in the execution of their task.

The members of the Commissariat shall not exercise any other professional activity during their terms of office.

For a period of three years immediately following the termination of his said term of office, no former member of the Commissariat shall engage in any professional activity which the Court, before which he or the Council may have brought the question, may declare to be incompatible with obligations resulting from his tenure of office because of its connection with the functions of such office. In case of violation of this provision, the Court may decree the forfeiture of the pension rights of the person concerned.

Article 21

1. The members of the Commissariat shall be appointed by agreement between the governments of the Member States.

2. The members appointed for the first time following the entry of the Treaty into effect shall hold office for a period of three years following their appointment.

In case a vacancy should occur during this first period for one of the reasons set forth in Article 22 hereinafter, such vacancy shall be filled in accordance with the provisions of Section 1 of this Article.

The same procedure shall apply to the general reappointment rendered necessary in case Paragraph 2 of Article 36 hereinafter should be applied.

3. At the expiration of the initial period of three years, a general reappointment shall take place.

4. Thereafter, one-third of the members of the Commissariat shall be reappointed every two years.

Immediately after the general reappointment provided for in Paragraph 3 of this Article, the Council shall determine by lot the members whose terms of office shall end respectively after the first and after the second two-year periods.

5. If the members of the Commissariat should resign from their offices pursuant to the provisions of Paragraph 2, Article 36, hereinafter, the provisions of Paragraphs 3 and 4 of this Article shall be applicable.

Article 22

Apart from routine replacements, the duties of individual members of the Commissariat shall terminate on death, resignation or dismissal.

A deceased, resigned or removed member shall be replaced, for the remaining period of his term of office, in accordance with the provisions of Article 21 hereinabove. There shall be no replacement if the remaining period of such member's term of office is less than three months.

Article 23

Any member of the Commissariat, if he no longer fulfills the conditions necessary for the performance of his duties, or if he has been guilty of serious misdemeanor, may be compulsorily retired by the Court on request by the Council or the Commissariat.

In such a case, the Council, by unanimous vote, may temporarily suspend such a member from the Commissariat and provide for his replacement until such time as the Court shall be acted.

Article 24

1. Decisions of the Commissariat are taken by a majority of members present. The President shall cast tie-breaking votes. Nevertheless, no decision may be taken by fewer than four affirmative votes.

2. The internal regulations shall fix the quorum. The quorum shall be of no fewer than five members.

3. Should the Council, pursuant to the provisions of Paragraph 1 of Article 20, decide to reduce the number of members of the Commissariat, it shall, under the same conditions, appropriately modify the figures set forth in the two preceding paragraphs of this Article.

Article 25

1. The Governments of the member States shall appoint the President of the Commissariat from among its membership by agreement among themselves.

The President's term of office shall be four years. He shall be eligible for reappointment. His term of office may end under the same circumstances as that of the members of the Commissariat.

2. The President shall not be included in any determination by lot which could result in abridging his term of office as President by causing the expiration of his term of office as a member of the Commissariat.

When the President is chosen from among members of the Commissariat already in office, the length of his term of office as a member of the Commissariat shall be extended until the expiration of his term of office as President.

3. Except in the case of a general reappointment, the President shall be designated after consultation with the members of the Commissariat.

Article 25 bis

1. The term of office of the first President shall end after a period of three years.

Article 26

1. The Commissariat shall establish general organisational regulations which will determine specifically:

a. On the basis of the principal Board, the categories of decisions which should be taken collectively by the Commissariat and those which might be delegated to members of the Commissariat to be taken individually within their respective field of competence. within their respective field of competence.

b. The allocation of the tasks of the Commissariat among its members, bearing in mind the necessity for a stable structure while at the same time leaving open the possibility for changes which experience may demonstrate to be necessary; this allocation shall not necessarily correspond to the number of members of the Commissariat.

2. Within the framework of these regulations:

a. The Commissariat shall determine the respective duties of its members;

b. The President:

— shall coordinate the performance of these duties;

— shall insure the implementation of decisions; and shall be responsible for the administration of the services.

In the case and under the conditions provided for in Article 123 hereinafter, the President may be temporarily vested with special powers.

Article 27

In the exercise of its powers, the Commissariat shall take decisions, make recommendations and issue opinions.

Decisions shall be binding in all their constituent elements.

Recommendations shall be binding with respect to the objectives which they specify, but shall leave to those to whom they are directed the choice of appropriate means for attaining these objectives.

Opinions shall not be binding.

In cases in which the Commissariat is empowered to issue a decision, it may limit itself to making a recommendation.

Article 28

All decisions and recommendations as well as all opinions of the Commissariat shall be published or notified in accordance with rules laid down by the Council.

Decisions, recommendations or opinions of the Commissariat directed to the Government of a member State shall be addressed to the authority designated for this purpose by the said State.

Article 29

The Commissariat shall report to the Council at regular intervals.

It shall supply the Council with information requested of it by the Council and shall undertake studies at its request.

The Commissariat and the Council shall exchange information and hold reciprocal consultations.

Article 30

The Commissariat shall have at its disposal the civilian and military personnel necessary to permit it to assume all the tasks assigned to it by the present Treaty.

The Services which the Commissariat establishes for this purpose, civilian as well as military, shall be responsible to it by the same authority and on the same level.

Article 31

1. Ranks higher than those of Commander of a basic unit of homogeneous nationality shall be conferred by decision of the Commissariat on approval by the Council acting unanimously.

2. For a temporary period, ranks in the units of homogeneous nationality of the European Defence Forces, and all other ranks, shall be conferred, at the option of each member State,

— either by the appropriate national authority upon the recommendation of the Commissariat;

— or by the Commissariat upon recommendation coming through the appropriate chain of command, after consultation with national authorities.

3. a. Assignments of Commanders of basic units, of general officers to posts involving the exercise of authority over elements of various nationalities, and assignments to certain high positions with the Commissariat designated by the Council, shall be made by the Commissariat with the unanimous concurrence of the Council.

b. All other military assignments shall be made by the Commissariat, having due regard for the recommendations of appropriate command echelons.

4. Insofar as civilian positions are concerned, heads of services directly responsible to the Commissariat shall be appointed by the latter with the unanimous concurrence of the Council.

Article 32

The Commissariat shall assure all necessary liaison with the member States, with other States, and, in general, with all international organisations whose cooperation is needed in carrying out the objectives of the present Treaty.

Chapter II
The Assembly

Article 33

1. The Assembly of the European Defence Community is the Assembly provided for in Articles 20 and 21 of the Treaty of April 18, 1951 establishing the European Coal and Steel Community, supplemented as concerns respectively the German Federal Republic, France and Italy, by three delegates each, who shall be elected under the same conditions and for the same terms as the other delegates, and whose first terms of office shall expire at the same time as theirs.

The Assembly so supplemented shall exercise the powers so conferred on it by the present Treaty. If it deems it necessary, it may elect its own President and officials and draw up its own internal regulations.

2. If the Conference provided for in the last Paragraph of Article 38 hereinafter has not reached an agreement within one year after its being called into session, the member States by agreement among themselves shall proceed to a revision of the provisions of Paragraph 1 of this present Article without waiting for the Conference to finish its work.

Article 34

The Assembly shall hold an annual session. It shall meet under its own authority on the last Tuesday in October. The duration of the session shall not exceed one month.

The Assembly may be convened in an extraordinary session at the request of the Commissariat, the Council, the President of the Assembly or the majority of its members, or, in the case provided for in Article 46 hereinafter, at the request of a member State.

Article 34 bis

The Assembly shall meet one month after the date on which the Commissariat shall have assumed its functions; it shall be called into session by the Commissariat. The provisions of Article 34 relating to the duration of regular sessions of the Assembly shall not be applicable to the first session.

As soon as it meets, the Assembly shall be empowered to perform the duties assigned to it by the present Treaty, with the exception of voting on a motion of censure provided for in Paragraph 2 of Article 36 hereinafter; such a vote may only come at the end of one year following the date on which the Commissariat shall have assumed its functions.

Article 35

The members of the Commissariat may attend all sessions of the Assembly. The President or any members of the Commissariat designated by the Commissariat for this purpose shall be heard upon their request. The Commissariat shall reply, orally or in writing, to questions which are put by the Assembly or by its members.

The members of the Council may attend all sessions and shall be heard on their request.

Article 36

1. Each year the Commissariat shall submit to the Assembly a general report concerning the former's activity, which shall be presented one month before the opening of the regular session. The Assembly shall discuss this report and may formulate comments and express its wishes and suggestions.

2. If a motion of censure concerning the operations of the Commissariat is presented to the Assembly, a vote may be taken thereon only after a period of not less than three

days following the introduction of such motion, and such vote shall be by roll call.

Should the motion of censure be carried by a two-thirds majority of the votes cast and by a majority of the members of the Assembly, the members of the Commissariat must collectively resign. They shall continue to transact current business until steps have been taken to replace them under the conditions laid down in Article 21 above.

Article 37

The Assembly shall adopt its own internal rules of procedure by vote of a majority of its membership.

Records of Proceedings of the Assembly shall be published in the circumstances and under the conditions which the Assembly shall define.

Article 38

1. Within the period provided for in Section 2 of this Article, the Assembly shall study:

a. the constitution of an Assembly of the European Defence Community elected on a democratic basis;

b. the powers which might be granted to such an Assembly;

c. any changes which might have to be made to the provisions of the present Treaty concerning the other institutions of the Community, more particularly with a view to ensuring that the States shall be suitably represented.

In its work, the Assembly will particularly bear in mind the following principles:

The permanent organisation which will replace the present provisional organisation should be so conceived as to be able to constitute one of the elements in a subsequent federal or confederal structure, based on the principle of the separation of powers and having, in particular, a two-chamber system of representation.

The Assembly shall also examine problems arising from the co-existence of different agencies for European cooperation already established, or which might be established, with a view to ensuring coordination within the framework of the federal or confederal structure.

2. The proposals of the Assembly shall be submitted to the Council within six months from the date on which the Assembly shall have assumed its functions. These proposals will then be forwarded, together with the opinion of the Council, by the President of the Assembly to the Governments of the member States, which, within three months from the date of the receipt of these proposals, shall call a conference for the purpose of examining such proposals.

Chapter III
The Council

Article 39

1. The general task of the Council is to harmonise the actions of the Commissariat with the policies of the Governments of the member States.

2. The Council may, within the framework of the present Treaty, issue directives for the action of the Commissariat.

These directives shall be issued by unanimous vote. Concerning matters which have not been the subject of directives by the Council, the Commissariat may take action, subject to the provisions of the present Treaty, with a view to ensuring the attainment of the objectives of the present Treaty.

3. In accordance with the provisions of the present Treaty, the Council:

a. shall take decisions;

b. shall issue concurrences which the Commissariat shall be bound to obtain before making decisions or issuing recommendations.

4. Unless otherwise provided in the present Treaty, the decisions of the Council shall be taken and its opinions issued by simple majority.

5. Whenever the Council is consulted by the Commissariat, it shall deliberate without necessarily proceeding to a vote. The minutes of these deliberations shall be transmitted to the Commissariat.

Article 40

The Council shall be composed of representatives of the member States.

Each member State shall designate thereto a member of its Government who may be represented by a Deputy.

The Council shall be organised so as to be able to exercise its functions at all times. To this end, each member State shall at all times have a representative able to participate in the deliberations of the Council without delay.

The Presidency of the Council shall be assumed for a term of three months by each member of the Council by rotation in the alphabetical order of the member States.

Article 41

The Council shall meet as often as may be necessary and at least once every three months. It shall be convened by its Chairman, either on his own initiative or at the request of a member of the Council or of the Commissariat.

Article 41 bis

The Council shall meet as soon as the present Treaty shall have entered into effect.

Article 42

When a vote is taken, a member of the Council may act as proxy for not more than one other member.

Article 43

1. In cases where the present Treaty requires concurrence or decision of the Council by simple majority, such concurrence or decision shall be made if it is carried:

— either by an absolute majority of the representatives of the member States;

— or, in case of an equal division of votes, by the votes of representatives of the member States which together place at the disposal of the Community at least two-thirds of the total contributions of the member States.

2. In cases where the present Treaty requires concurrence or decision of the Council by a qualified majority, such concurrence or decision shall be made:

— either by the majority specified if such majority includes the votes of the representatives of the member States which together place at the disposal of the Community at least two-thirds of the total contributions of the member States;

— or if it receives the votes of the representatives of five member States.

3. In cases where the present Treaty requires concurrence or decision of the Council by unanimous vote, such concurrence or decision shall be made if it is approved by the votes of all the members present or represented at the Council; abstentions shall not

prevent the adoption of such concurrence of decision.

4. In Paragraphs 1 and 2 of this Article, the word 'contributions' shall be understood to mean the average between the percentage of the financial contributions actually paid during the previous fiscal year and the percentage of men making up the European Defence Forces on the first day of the current semester.

Article 43 bis

1. For the purposes of the application of Paragraph 4 of Article 43 hereinabove, until the date set for the execution of the plan for the formation of the first echelon of the forces, the average of contributions furnished by the member States, which is referred to in the said Paragraph, shall be evaluated on a forfeitary basis as follows:

Germany	3
Belgium	2
France	3
Italy	3
Luxembourg	1
The Netherlands	2

2. During the transitional period defined in Paragraph 1 of this Article, the requirement of a percentage of the total contributions of the member States established by Article 43, Paragraph 1 hereinabove shall be considered to have been met whenever at least nine-fourteenths of the total value of the contributions of the member States as evaluated on a forfeitary basis is reached.

Article 44

Regulations defining or modifying the status of personnel, general organisation, recruitment rules, and the size and structure of forces, as well as modifications in the plan establishing the European Defence Forces, shall be made by unanimous agreement of the Council, upon the proposal of a member of the Council or of the Commissariat, and shall be executed by the latter.

Article 45

The Council shall determine the salary, emoluments and pension rights of the President and members of the Commissariat.

Article 46

The Council, acting by a two-thirds majority, may, on the initiative of one of its members, invite the Commissariat to take any measure falling within its competence.

If the Commissariat does not act on such invitation, the Council or a member State may refer the matter to the Assembly for purposes of action under Paragraph 2, Article 36 hereinabove.

Article 47

The Council shall decide whether it is appropriate to call a joint meeting with the Council of the North Atlantic Treaty Organisation and the Council of the Community.

Decisions taken unanimously in the course of joint meetings of the two Councils shall be binding on the institutions of the Community.

Article 48
The decision of the Council provided for in Paragraph 4 of the Protocol Concerning Relations between the North Atlantic Treaty Organisation and the European Defence Community shall be taken unanimously.

Article 49
The minutes of the meetings of the Council shall be transmitted to the member States and to the Commissariat.

Article 50
The Council shall establish its own rules of procedure.

Chapter IV
The Court

Article 51
The Court shall ensure the rule of law in the interpretation and application of the present Treaty and implementing regulations.

Article 52
The Court shall be the Court of Justice of the European Coal and Steel Community.

Article 53
In the discharge of its functions, the Court shall, in the cases and in the manner provided for in the jurisdictional Protocol and Statute, referred to in Article 67, be assisted by a legal system including specifically subordinate courts which shall be European in character.

Article 54
1. The Court shall have jurisdiction to hear appeals from decisions or recommendations of the Commissariat, by a member State, by the Council or by the Assembly on grounds of lack of legal competence, substantial procedural violations, violation of the present Treaty or of any rule relating to its application, or abuse of power.

2. Appeals must be taken within a maximum period of one month following either the publication or notification of the decision or recommendation.

3. If the Court should pronounce a judgment of annulment, the matter shall be remanded to the Commissariat which shall take the measures necessary to give effect to the judgment of annulment.

Article 55
1. If the Commissariat is required by a provision of the present Treaty or of implementing regulations to issue a decision or recommendation and fails to fulfill this obligation, such omission shall be brought to its attention by the member States or by the Council.

The same shall apply if the Commissariat refrains from issuing a decision or recommendation which it is empowered to issue by a provision of the present Treaty or of implementing regulations where such failure to act constitutes a misuse of power.

2. If at the end of a period of two months the Commissariat has not issued any decision

or recommendation, an appeal may be brought before the Court, within a period of one month, against the implicit negative decision which is presumed to result from such inaction.

Article 56

1. If a member State feels that, in a given case, an action or lack of action on the part of the Commissariat may provoke, as concerns such State, fundamental and persistent disturbances, it may so inform the Commissariat.

After consulting with the Council, the Commissariat shall, if appropriate, recognise the existence of such a situation and decide upon the measures to be taken under the provisions of the present Treaty to end such a situation while at the same time safeguarding the essential interests of the Community. The Commissariat shall make its decision within a two-week period.

2. If an appeal based on the provisions of this Article is made to the Court against the decision or against the explicit or implicit decision refusing to recognise the existence of the situation indicated hereinabove, the Court shall decide on the merits of the case and shall provisionally take all necessary measures.

3. If a decision of the Commissariat is annulled, the latter shall decide upon measures to be taken to achieve the ends provided for in Paragraph 1, Subparagraph 2 of this Article within the framework of the decree of the Court.

Article 57

1. The Court shall have jurisdiction to hear appeals from decisions of the Council by a member State, by the Commissariat or by the Assembly on grounds of lack of legal competence, substantial procedural violations, violation of the present Treaty or of any rule of law relating to its applications, or misuse of power.

2. Such appeals must be taken within one month following the date on which the decision of the Council is transmitted to the member States or to the Commissariat.

Article 58

1. The Court may annul decisions of the Assembly on the motion of the member State or of the Commissariat.

The jurisdiction of the Court may be invoked for such an appeal only on grounds of lack of legal competence to act or of substantial procedural violations.

2. The jurisdiction of the Court shall be invoked for such an appeal within a period of one month following the date of publication of the Assembly's decision in question.

Article 59

Appeals to the Court shall not have the effect of a stay.

However, if in its judgment circumstances demand it, the Court may order a stay in the execution of the decision or recommendation in question.

The Court may prescribe any other necessary provisional measures.

Article 60

The Court shall have jurisdiction, in the cases and in the manner provided for in the jurisdictional Protocol and Statute referred to in Article 67, to hear controversies concerning the civil liability of the Community and the status of its agents.

Article 61
The Court shall have jurisdiction to hear criminal matters in the cases and in the manner provided for in the jurisdictional Protocol and Statute referred to in Article 67.

Article 61 bis
Transitional provisions contained in the jurisdictional Protocol shall be applicable until such time as a common military criminal code comes into effect.

Article 62
Without prejudice to the provisions of the jurisdictional Statute provided for in Article 67, the Court is the only authority competent to give rulings, of a prejudicial nature, on the validity of decisions or recommendations of the Commissariat and of the proceedings of the Council, should a dispute brought before a national court question their validity.

Article 63
The Court shall have jurisdiction, in the cases and in the manner provided for in its Statute, to pass, in virtue of an arbitration clause contained in a public or private law contract to which the Community is a party or which is undertaken on its behalf.

Article 64
The Court shall have jurisdiction in any other case provided for in an additional clause to the present Treaty.

The Court may also exercise jurisdiction in all cases relating to the objectives of the present Treaty, where the laws of a member State grant such jurisdiction to it.

Article 65
1. Any dispute among the member States concerning the application of the present Treaty which cannot be settled by other means may be submitted to the Court either at the common request of States which are parties to the dispute or at the request of one of the States.

2. The Court shall also have jurisdiction over any disputes among the member States relating to the objectives of the present Treaty if such disputes are submitted to it pursuant to a compromise agreement.

Article 66
Judgments of the Court shall be enforceable on the territories of the member States.

Enforcement of such judgments on the territory of a member State shall be in accordance with the laws in force in such State; in particular, there may be no enforcement of such a judgment against a member State except to the extent and by the means permitted by the legislative provisions of such State.

Enforcement of judgments of the Court shall take place after the judgment formula in use in the territory of the State concerned has been appended; no other action shall be necessary with respect to a judgment of the Court other than verification of its authenticity. These formalities with respect to the judgments of the Court shall be carried out by a Minister designated for that purpose by each of the Governments.

Article 67
The implementation of the provisions of this chapter and of the Jurisdictional Protocol

shall be regulated by a Jurisdictional Statute which shall be enacted in the form of a convention among the member States and which shall, in particular, make the modifications necessary to ensure such application in the Statute of the Court as annexed to the Treaty establishing the European Coal and Steel Community.

Title III
Military Provisions

Chapter I
Organisation and Administration of the European Defence Forces

Article 68

1. The basic units, in which the operational duties of the various Arms of the Land Forces will have to be combined, shall be composed of elements of a single nationality. These basic units shall be as small as is compatible with the principle of their effectiveness. They shall be relieved to the maximum degree possible of logistic functions and shall depend on higher integrated echelons for their supplies and maintenance.

2. The Army Corps shall be composed of basic units of different national origins, except in special cases resulting from tactical needs or organisational necessities and determined by the Commissariat on the recommendation of the competent Supreme Commander responsible to the North Atlantic Treaty Organisation with the unanimous concurrence of the Council. Their tactical support units as well as their logistic support formations shall be of the integrated type; but constituent units of regiment or battalion size remain homogeneous and their allotment among nationalities shall be made according to the proportion existing among the basic ground units. The Command and Headquarters of the Army Corps shall be integrated; such integration shall be effected in the manner best suited to ensuring effectiveness in their utilisation.

3. The basic units and their support troops and services may occasionally be brought into Army Corps subject to the authority of the North Atlantic Treaty Organisation, and reciprocally, divisions subject to the authority of the North Atlantic Treaty Organisation may be brought into European Army Corps.

The Commanding echelons of Forces subject to the authority of the North Atlantic Treaty Organisation, to which the European units shall be attached organically, shall integrate elements coming from these units and vice-versa.

Article 69

1. The basic Air Force Units shall be composed of elements of the same national origin, each of which shall have homogeneous combat matériel corresponding to a given basic mission.

These basic units shall, as far as possible, be relieved of their logistic functions and shall depend upon higher integrated echelons for their operation and maintenance.

2. A certain number of basic units of different national origins shall be grouped under the orders of the integrated type higher echelons, except in special cases resulting from tactical needs or organisational necessities and determined by the Commissariat on the recommendation of the competent Supreme Commander responsible to the North Atlantic Treaty Organisation with the unanimous concurrence of the Council. The logistic

support formations shall be integrated; but the constituent service units shall remain of homogeneous national composition and their allotment among nationalities shall be made according to the proportion existing among the basic Units.

3. European basic units as well as their support units may be brought under Commands responsible to the North Atlantic Treaty Organisation and, reciprocally, basic units subject to the authority of the North Atlantic Treaty Organisation may be brought under European Commands.

The Command echelons responsible to the North Atlantic Treaty Organisation to which European units are attached organically shall integrate European elements and vice-versa.

Article 70

1. The European Naval Forces shall consist of formations which are assigned to the protection of the maritime approaches of the European territories of member States, determined by agreement between the governments.

2. The contingents of the European naval forces shall form groups of homogeneous nationality and European status suitable for a single tactical task.

3. These groupings may occasionally, wholly or in part, be incorporated into formations subject to the authority of the North Atlantic Treaty Organisation; thenceforth, elements furnished by the groupings shall be integrated into the command echelons of such formations.

Article 71

With the unanimous concurrence of the Council, the Commissariat shall establish the plans for the organisation of the Forces. The Commissariat shall ensure the implementation of such plans.

Article 72

1. Personnel conscripted to serve in the European Defence Forces shall serve the same period of active duty.

2. The period of active duty service in the European Defence Forces shall be rendered uniform as soon as possible by unanimous decision of the Council on recommendation of the Commissariat.

Article 73

1. Recruitment for the European Defence Forces in each member State shall be carried out in accordance with laws of such State within the framework of the common principles defined in the Military Protocol.

2. The Commissariat shall supervise the recruiting operations for the European Defence Forces carried out by the member States in accordance with the provisions of the present Treaty, and, in order to ensure conformity with such provisions, shall, if necessary, make recommendations to the member States.

3. Beginning with the date fixed by common agreement among the governments of the member States, the Commissariat shall itself undertake recruiting in accordance with the provisions of such agreement and within the framework of the common principles laid down in the Military Protocol.

Article 74

1. The Commissariat shall direct the training and preparation of the European Defence Forces according to a common doctrine and uniform methods. In particular, the

Commissariat shall direct the schools of the Community.

2. Upon the request of a member State, due regard shall be had, in the application of the principles enumerated in Paragraph 1 of this Article, to the particular situation resulting for such State from the existence, by virtue of the Constitution, of more than one official language.

Article 75

The Commissariat shall draw up mobilisation plans for the European Defence Forces, in consultation with the Governments of the member States.

Without prejudice to the final organisation referred to in the provisions of Article 38 hereinabove, the decision to proceed with mobilisation shall be made by the member States; execution of mobilisation measures shall be divided between the Community and the member States in a manner to be determined by agreements between the Commissariat and the said States.

Article 76

The Commissariat shall make such inspections and undertake such supervisions as may be necessary.

Article 77

1. The Commissariat shall determine the territorial deployment of the European Defence Forces within the framework of recommendations of the competent Supreme Commander responsible to the North Atlantic Treaty Organisation. In case of differences of opinion which cannot be settled with the latter, the Commissariat may set aside such recommendations only with the unanimous approval of the Council.

Within the framework of the general decisions provided for in Subparagraph 1 of this Article, the Commissariat shall take executive measures, after consultation with the State in which the troops are to be stationed.

2. In case of differences of opinion on essential points, the State in question may appeal to the Council. Such State must abide by the decision of the Commissariat if the Council upholds the latter by a two-thirds majority vote.

The privilege granted member States by Article 56 hereinabove shall not be affected by the provisions of this Article.

Article 78

The Commissariat shall administer personnel and equipment in conformance with the provisions of the present Treaty.

It shall endeavour to ensure a distribution of armaments and equipment tending towards uniformity within units of the European Defence Forces.

Article 78 bis

1. As soon as it begins to function, the Commissariat shall:

— draw up plans for the formation and equipment of the first echelon of the Forces in accordance with the provisions of an agreement adopted by the member States and within the framework of North Atlantic Treaty Organisation plans;

— decide upon and organise the assistance to be requested from States parties to the North Atlantic Treaty for the training of contingents;

— draw up summary provisional regulations on essential points.

2. As soon as it takes up its duties, the Commissariat shall undertake formation of

the units of the first echelon of Forces.

3. As soon as the Treaty comes into effect, the units already in existence and the contingents to be recruited by the member States to complete this first echelon shall come under the authority of the Community and shall be placed under the jurisdiction of the Commissariat, which shall exercise over them the powers granted it by the present Treaty, under the conditions provided for in the Military Protocol.

4. The Commissariat shall submit to the Council as soon as possible the plans and projects provided for in Paragraph 1 of this Article.

The Council shall approve:
— unanimously, the plan for forming the first echelon of the Forces;
— by a two-thirds majority, all other texts.

Such texts shall be put into effect by the Commissariat as soon as they have been approved by the Council.

Article 79

A single regulation concerning general military discipline, which shall be applicable to the members of the European Defence Forces, shall be enacted by agreement among the Governments of the member States, ratified in accordance with the constitutional procedures of each such State.

Chapter II
Legal Status of the European Defence Forces

Article 80

1. In the exercise of the functions assigned to it by the present Treaty, and without prejudice to the rights and obligations of the member States:
— the Community shall have, in respect of the European Defence Forces and their members, the same rights and obligations as the States in respect of their national forces and their members, in accordance with customary international law;
— the Community shall respect the rules embodied in conventions concerning the rules of warfare which bind one or more of its member States.

2. Consequently, European Defence Forces and their members shall benefit, under international law, by the same treatment as national forces and their members.

Article 81

1. The Community shall ensure that the European Defence Forces and their members conform in their conduct to the rules of international law. It shall ensure the punishment of any violation of such rules which may be committed by such Forces or their members.

2. The Community shall take, within the limits of its competence, penal measures and all other appropriate measures in all cases in which such a violation shall have been committed by the Forces of a third State or their members.

The member States shall likewise, on their part, within the limits of their competence, take penal measures and all other appropriate measures against all violations of rules of international law committed against the European Defence Forces or their members.

Article 82

The status of the European Defence Forces shall be determined by a special Protocol.

Title IV
Financial Provisions

Article 83

The financial administration of the European Defence Community shall be carried out in accordance with the provisions of the present Treaty, the Financial Protocol and the financial regulations.

To ensure the respect of the provisions thus set forth, a Financial Controller and a Board of Auditors shall be created whose powers and responsibilities are defined in the following Articles.

Article 84

The Financial Controller shall be independent of the Commissariat and responsible to the Council. He shall be appointed by unanimous vote of the Council. His term of office shall be five years. He may be reappointed.

Article 85

The Board of Auditors shall be an independent collegial authority. Nationals of each of the member States shall be among its members.

The Council shall, by unanimous vote, determine the number of members of the Board. The Council shall by two-thirds vote appoint members of the Board and its President. The term of office of members of the Board shall be five years. They may be reappointed.

Article 86

As soon as the Treaty comes into effect, all the revenues and all the expenditures of the Community shall be written into a common annual budget.

The fiscal year of the Community shall last one calendar year and shall begin on 1 January. This date may be changed by decision of the Council.

Article 87

1. In consultation with the Governments of the member States and having regard especially for the provisions of Article 71, the Commissariat shall prepare the budget of the Community. The draft of a common plan for armament, equipment, supply and infrastructure shall be annexed to the draft budget.

The individual revenues and expenditures of the institutions of the Community shall be dealt with in special sections within the general budget.

2. This draft shall be submitted to the Council at least three months before the beginning of the fiscal year.

Within a period of one month, the Council shall decide:

   a. By a unanimous vote, the total size of the budget authorisations and appropriations, and the amount of the contribution of each member State determined in conformity with Article 94 below. It will be the responsibility of the Government of each member State to ensure that the contribution is entered in the budget of that State in accordance with the requirements of its Constitution;

   b. By a two-thirds majority, the distribution of expenditures.

The provisions of Subparagraphs *a* and *b* of this Paragraph shall not be applicable to the receipts and expenditures resulting from an agreement concerning foreign aid provided for in Article 99 hereinafter, nor to revenues and expenditures which merely transit through the common budget as provided in the Financial Protocol.

3. The common budget thus approved by the Council shall be forwarded to the Assembly, which shall take a vote on it not later than two weeks before the beginning of the fiscal year.

The Assembly may propose changes by annulling, reducing, increasing, or creating revenues or expenditures. These proposals may not have the effect of increasing the total amount of expenditures appearing in the budget adopted by the Council.

The Assembly, by a two-thirds majority of votes cast and a simple majority of its membership, may propose the rejection of the entire budget.

4. In all cases provided for in Paragraph 3 of this Article, the Commissariat or a member State may, within fifteen days after the vote, ask the Council to undertake a second reading within two weeks. Proposals of the Assembly shall be adopted if the Council upon such a request approves them by a two-thirds majority. If the Council has not been requested to undertake a second reading as herein provided within a fifteen-day period, the Assembly's proposal shall be considered as having been adopted by the Council.

Article 87 bis

1. Notwithstanding the provisions of Article 87 hereinabove, the Council alone shall approve the budget for the period between the entry into effect of the Treaty and the end of the calendar year in question.

In the matter of expenditures, the military and financial programmes of all of the member States for the build-up of units which are to constitute the European Forces shall be taken into account to the greatest extent possible in establishing this budget.

2. For the execution of this budget, the Commissariat shall delegate to the appropriate national services the responsibility of carrying out, on its behalf, the expenditures for the European Defence Forces, to the extent that its own services do not allow it to perform these tasks.

3. Until the first common budget has been approved, the Community shall receive advances from the member States to enable it to meet its first expenses; these advances shall be credited later to their contributions. Expenditures paid out of these advances shall be reinstated in the common budget.

4. The budget for the fiscal year following the fiscal year defined in Paragraph 1 of this Article shall be prepared, approved and executed according to the principles of this Treaty.

However:

a. The contributions of the member States to the budget for this fiscal year shall be determined in accordance with the procedure adopted by the North Atlantic Treaty Organisation, to the exclusion of any other method of distribution;

b. At the request of any member State which feels that the common budget thus drawn up is not in accord with the intentions expressed by its Government or its Parliament, either as regards the fulfillment of its commitments to the North Atlantic Treaty Organisation or the means employed to carry out these commitments, the Community shall submit this budget to the competent authorities of the North Atlantic Treaty Organisation for their opinion.

Article 88

1. If, at the beginning of the fiscal year, the budget has not yet been finally approved, the Community shall be empowered to provide for its expenditures by monthly slices equal to 1/12 of the funds in the budget for the preceding year. This power shall end

after three months following the beginning of the fiscal year. The expenditures may not exceed one fourth of expenditures for the preceding year.

In the case provided for in the preceding Subparagraph, the member States shall grant advances to the Community in accordance with the scale applicable in the preceding fiscal year. These advances shall be credited against their contributions.

If at the expiration of the time limit provided for in the first Subparagraph, the budget has not yet finally entered into force, the budget decided on by the Council shall enter into force, provided that the Assembly has had at least two weeks' time to study it.

2. In case of necessity, the Commissariat may, during the course of the fiscal year, submit a supplementary draft budget which shall be approved in the same manner as the regular budget with the time limits reduced by half.

Article 89

1. The budget shall be subdivided into sections, chapters and articles. It shall be established in gross totals and shall contain all the revenues and all the expenditures of the Community.

In particular, it shall include the annual expenditures necessary for the execution of common plans for armament, equipment, supply and infrastructure for a period of several fiscal years.

2. The budget shall be established in a common currency chosen by the Council by a two-thirds majority.

The relation between this common currency and the national currency shall be determined by the official rate of exchange indicated to the Community by each State.

Article 90

1. The Commissariat may, within the limits of general or specific authorisations given it in the budget itself by a two-thirds majority of the Council or by the financial regulations, inter-transfer appropriations among the items of the budget for the administration of which it is responsible. Such transfers shall require the approval of the Financial Controller whenever they are made by virtue of a general authorisation.

2. Under the same conditions, similar transfer powers shall be vested in other institutions of the Community with respect to appropriations for the administration of which they are responsible.

Article 91

The execution of the budget shall be ensured by the Commissariat and by the other institutions of the Community in accordance with the provisions of the Financial Protocol.

In the establishment and execution of the budget, the institutions of the Community shall ensure that commitments taken by the member States with the North Atlantic Treaty Organisation are respected. Contracts made by the member States with third parties before the Treaty comes into force shall be executed unless they can be modified in the interest of the Community with the accord of the Government which signed them.

Article 92

The execution of the budget shall be supervised by the Financial Controller.

All decisions of the Commissariat which commit expenditures shall be submitted for approval to the Financial Controller, who, by his signature, shall verify the budgetary regularity of the expenditure and its conformity with provisions of the financial regulations.

Without prejudice to the provisions of Articles 54 and 57 hereinabove, the Commissariat may override a refusal to approve by the Financial Controller, by sending the latter, in writing, a special requisition for the expenditure in question. After having received this requisition, the Controller shall immediately report it to the Council; the latter shall consider the matter with the least possible delay.

At the expiration of any three months period, the Financial Controller shall send a report on the execution of the budget to the Council, which shall transmit it to the Assembly. This report shall contain all appropriate observations concerning the financial management of the Commissariat.

The Financial Controller shall give his opinion on the budget drafts. This opinion shall be transmitted to the Commissariat. The Council shall add this opinion to the budget which it shall submit to the Assembly.

Article 93

The revenues of the Community shall include:

    a. the contributions paid by the member States;

    b. revenues of the Community itself;

    c. the sums which the Community may receive by virtue of Articles 7 hereinabove and 99 hereinafter.

The Community shall also have at its disposal any contribution in kind received by virtue of these same articles.

Article 94

As soon as the Treaty enters into effect, the contributions of the member States shall be fixed by the Council in accordance with the procedure adopted by the North Atlantic Treaty Organisation.

The Council shall seek a method proper for the determination of the contributions which will ensure an equitable distribution of charges, taking into account principally the financial, economic and social capabilities of the member States. This method shall be adopted unanimously by the Council and shall be applied beginning with the first fiscal year following its approval.

If there is no agreement on such a method, the contributions will continue to be determined in accordance with the procedure adopted by the North Atlantic Treaty Organisation.

Article 95

1. The contributions, determined in accordance with the preceding Articles, shall be payable by 1/12 in the national currency, on the first day of each month. The Council, by unanimous decision, may accept the settlement by a State of its contribution in a currency other than its national currency.

2. In case of modification of the rate of exchange, the amounts remaining due on a contribution shall be adjusted on the basis of the new rate. However, as concerns sums corresponding to such adjustment, the debtor State may request that the total of such sums be limited to the loss suffered by the Community as a result of the modification in the rate of exchange. Such limitation shall be determined by unanimous decision of the Council.

The member States shall bear the entire burden of any additional expenditures on the Community's contracts which might result from the application of arrangements made by a member State in favour of contracting parties upon the occasion of a monetary reform.

3. If, in the course of the implementation of a budget, the real purchasing power of the currency of a member State becomes substantially inferior in comparison with the real purchasing power of the currencies of the other member States, without official modification of the rate of exchange, the Council, at the request of the Commissariat or of a member State, shall study the measures to be taken to compensate for the loss which such a change may bring to the Community.

Article 96
In the establishment and execution of the budget, the Community shall endeavour to limit the monetary transfer among the member States or between them and other countries, which might affect the economic and monetary stability of the member States.

The financial regulation will indicate the method by which such monetary transfers shall be carried out.

If, as a result of the execution of the budget, the economic and monetary stability of a member State should be affected, the Commissariat, at the request of that State and in agreement with the interested Governments, shall take the necessary corrective measures. If no agreement is reached on such measures, the Council, at the request of the Commissariat or of a member State, shall take the necessary steps as provided for in the present Treaty.

The member States commit themselves to make more flexible in favour of the Community the restrictions imposed by their exchange legislation on international monetary transfers.

Article 97
1. The Board of Auditors shall verify accounts in accordance with the provisions of the financial regulation.

On the basis of vouchers, the Board of Auditors shall verify the regularity of operations and the proper use of appropriations in the budget of the Community. For this activity, it is authorised to request the assistance of the accounting agencies of the member States.

2. The report on the result of the auditing of accounts shall be presented to the Council, which shall transmit it to the Assembly not later than six months after the expiration of the fiscal year.

On the basis of this report, the Board of Auditors shall submit to the Council a proposal for the discharge of each institution from further responsibility concerning its financial management for the period in question. The Council shall adopt a position with regard to this proposal and shall present it to the Assembly, which shall act thereon.

The discharge shall be considered to have been granted unless it is refused by a two-thirds majority of votes cast and a simple majority of the Assembly membership.

Article 98
The Governments of the member States may ask the Financial Controller and the Board of Auditors for copies of vouchers and other supporting documents which they use in connection with their duties.

Article 99
The Commissariat shall deal with questions relating to external aid provided to the Community in the form of equipment or finance.

Any agreement concerning external aid furnished to the Community shall be subject to approval by the Council notwithstanding special provisions of the Financial Protocol concerning external aid.

The Community may, with the unanimous approval of the Council, grant aid to third States in order to achieve the purposes defined in Article 2 hereinabove.

External aid in equipment intended for the European Defence Forces which the Community or member States may receive shall be administered by the Commissariat.

The Council, by a two-thirds majority vote, shall be empowered to give general directives to the Commissariat in order to ensure that the latter's action concerning external aid does not endanger the economic, financial and social stability of one or more member States.

Article 100
The conditions of remuneration and the pension rights of the civilian and military personnel employed by the Community are set forth in a Protocol annexed to the present Treaty.

Title V
Economic Provisions

Article 101
The Commissariat shall prepare in consultation with the Governments of the member States, the common armament, equipment, supply and infrastructure programmes of the European Defence Forces, and shall, in accordance with the provisions of Article 91 hereinabove, ensure their execution.

Article 102
1. In preparing and executing the programmes, the Commissariat shall:

a.   utilise in the best way possible the technical and economic capabilities of each of the member States and avoid causing serious disturbances in the economies of any of them;

b.   take into account the amounts of contributions to be furnished by the member States, and respect the rules set forth in the present Treaty concerning monetary transfers;

c.   in collaboration with the appropriate bodies of the North Atlantic Treaty Organisation simplify and standardise armament, equipment, supplies and infrastructure as much and as rapidly as possible.

2. The Council may give general directives to the Commissariat within the framework of the principles set forth hereinabove. These directives shall be issued by a two-thirds majority vote.

Article 103
1. The expenditures necessary for the execution of the programmes shall be entered in the budget estimate, which shall include as an annex a statement indicating projected execution of the programmes as allocated by categories of products and by geographical areas. Approval of the budget shall be considered approval of these programmes.

2. The Commissariat is authorised to establish programmes extending over a period of several years. It shall submit these programmes to the Council and shall request approval in principle from this body of those parts of the programmes which involve financial commitments extending over several years. This approval shall be granted by a two-thirds majority.

Article 104

1. The Commissariat shall be responsible for the execution of the programmes in consultation with the Council and the Governments of the member States.

2. The Commissariat shall ensure the placing of contracts, and shall supervise their execution, deliveries and payments for construction, goods and services.

The Commissariat shall organise civilian services decentralised in such a manner that they can use the resources of each member State under the conditions most advantageous for the Community.

3. Contracts shall be placed only after calling for the most extensive possible competitive bidding except in cases in which military secrecy, technical factors and conditions of urgency defined in the regulation provided for in Paragraph 4 hereinbelow necessitate otherwise. Contracts shall be concluded after public or restricted bidding or without bidding (by mutual consent) with contractors capable of fulfilling the conditions, and who are not excluded from public bidding in their own country. Exclusions based on nationality shall not be recognised as concerns nationals of the member States.

Within the framework of the provisions of Article 102 hereinabove, orders must be placed with the lowest bidders.

4. The procedures for placing contracts, and supervising the execution, deliveries and payment for construction, goods and services shall be determined by regulations. These regulations shall be submitted by the Commissariat for the approval of the Council by a two-thirds majority vote. They may be amended by the same procedure.

5. Contracts above a certain amount shall be submitted by the Commissariat to a Contracts Commission including nationals of each of the member States.

If the Commissariat does not conform to the advice of the Contracts Commission, it shall present a report to the Council giving its reasons.

The procedure for application of this Article shall be determined by regulations.

These regulations shall be submitted by the Commissariat for the approval of the Council by a two-thirds majority vote. They may be amended by the same procedure.

6. In disputes arising from contracts concluded between the Community and third parties residing in one of the member States, the administrative or judicial nature of the controversy, the jurisdiction *ratione materiae* or *ratione loci* of an administrative or judicial tribunal as well as the applicable law shall be determined.

a. Where the dispute concerns real property, by the law of the place where the property is located;

b. In all other cases, by the place where the supplier resides.

This rule may be changed by agreements between the parties, except as concerns the administrative or judicial nature of the competent jurisdiction and jurisdiction *ratione materiae*.

The Commissariat shall not normally have recourse to such agreements except in special cases or in order to give jurisdiction to a court operating under the authority of the Community.

7. If the Commissariat determines in the execution of the programmes that national public policy or private practices or agreements tend to distort or restrain seriously normal competitive conditions, it shall appeal to the Council, which shall decide unanimously on measures to remedy the situation.

The Council may be appealed to under the same conditions by a member State.

The regulations provided for in Paragraphs 4 and 5 of Article 104 hereinabove shall be submitted to the approval of the Council within six months after the entry into effect of the present Treaty.

Until these regulations are enacted, the Commissariat shall ensure the awarding of contracts in conformity with the legislative or administrative provisions in effect in the member States.

Article 105

If the Commissariat determines that the execution of all or part of a programme meets with such difficulties that it cannot be executed, as a result, for instance, of an insufficient supply of raw materials, lack of equipment or plant or abnormally high prices, or that its execution cannot be ensured within the required time, it shall notify the Council and seek with it the means appropriate to eliminate those difficulties.

The Council by unanimous vote, in consultation with the Commissariat, shall decide on the measures to be taken.

In the absence of a unanimous decision of the Council on measures envisaged in the previous paragraph, the Commissariat, after consultation with the Governments concerned, shall make recommendations to them in order to ensure the placing and execution of orders within the time limits provided in the programmes and at prices not abnormally high, taking into account the necessity of sharing as equitably as possible the burdens resulting therefrom among the economies of the member countries. The Council, by a two-thirds majority, may give the Commissariat general directives relative to the preparation of such recommendations.

A member State receiving such a recommendation may, within a ten-day period, notify the Council which shall act thereon.

Article 106

The Commissariat shall prepare a common programme for scientific and technical research in military fields as well as means of execution of this programme. This programme shall be submitted to the Council for approval under the same conditions as the common programmes for armament, equipment, supply and infrastructure of the European Defence Forces.

The Commissariat shall ensure the execution of the common research programme.

Article 107

1. The production of war matériel, the import and export of war matériel originating in or destined for third countries, measures directly concerning facilities for the production of war matériel, as well as the manufacture of experimental models and technical research on war matériel, are prohibited, except as authorised under the terms of Paragraph 3 hereinafter.

The present Article shall be applied with due regard for the observance of the rules of International law which prohibit recourse to certain forms of warfare.

2. The categories of war matériel covered by the prohibitions of Paragraph 1 hereinabove are defined in Annex I attached to the present Article. This Annex may be modified by the Council on the recommendation of the Commissariat or of a member of the Council, by a two-thirds majority.

3. The Commissariat shall lay down by regulation the procedural rules for the application of the present Article and for granting of licences for the production, import and export, and for measures directly concerning facilities for the production of war matériel, as well as for the manufacture of experimental models and for research relating to war matériel.

4. The following provisions shall be applicable to the granting of licences by the Commissariat:

a.   The Commissariat shall not grant licences for items listed in Annex II attached to this Article in strategically exposed areas, except by unanimous decision of the Council;
b.   The Commissariat shall not authorise construction of new power plants for military purposes except in territories defined by agreement among the Governments of the member States. The Commissariat shall make such licences subject to the appointment by it of a permanent inspector to ensure adherence by the establishments in question to the provisions of this Article. The same procedure shall be applicable to short range guided missiles used for anti-aircraft defence, as these are defined in Paragraph IV (d) of Annex II;
c.   As concerns exports, the Commissariat shall grant licences if it considers that they are consistent with the needs, the internal security and the international commitments, if any, of the Community;
d.   In the case of the manufacture of experimental models and technical research concerning war matériel, licences shall be granted so long as the Commissariat does not feel that such manufacture or research might endanger the internal security of the Community, and unless other directives are given by the Council, as provided in Paragraph 2 of Article 39;
e.   The Commissariat shall grant general licences for the production, import, and export of war matériel required by armed forces of member States not part of the European Defence Forces, and to forces of associated States for whom member States assume defence responsibility. The Commissariat shall nevertheless ensure that the beneficiaries of such licences do not make use of them beyond their needs;
f.   The Commissariat shall grant general licences concerning products listed in Annex I, when these are destined for civilian purposes. The Commissariat shall at the same time ensure that the beneficiaries of such licences do not employ them for other than such civilian purposes.
5.   The regulations referred to in Paragraph 3 above shall be drafted by the Commissariat with the approval of the Council acting by a two-thirds majority. They may be amended with the approval of the Council acting by a two-thirds majority, on a proposal either by the Commissariat or by a member of the Council.
6.   At the request of the Commissariat, the Court may, under the conditions prescribed by the Jurisdictional Statute referred to in Article 67, decree the following penalties against persons or enterprises violating the provisions of this Article:
— In the case of production, import and export of war matériel, penalties and fines may be imposed not exceeding 50 times the value of the products concerned. This maximum may be either doubled or raised to the equivalent, in national currency, of 1 million money of account units in cases of recurrent or particularly serious offences;
— In case of technical research, the manufacture of experimental models, and measures facilitating directly the production of war matériel, penalties not exceeding, in national currency, the equivalent of 100,000 money of account units may be imposed. This amount may be raised to the equivalent in national currency, of 1 million money of account units in cases of recurrent or particularly serious offences.

Annex I to Article 107

1   *War weapons*
a.   Portable firearms, with the exception of hunting weapons and calibres less than 7mm.
b.   Machine guns.
c.   Anti-tank weapons

    d. Artillery and mortars.
    e. Anti-aircraft weapons (D.C.A.).
    f. Smoke-screen, gas and flame producing apparatuses.
2. *Munitions and rockets of all types for military use.*
    a. Munitions for war weapons defined in Paragraph 1 hereinabove and grenades.
    b. Self-propelled weapons.
    c. Torpedoes of all types.
    d. Mines of all types.
    e. Bombs of all types.
3. *Powder and explosives for military use, including matériel primarily used for propulsions by rockets.*
    Exempted will be products principally for civilian use, specifically:
        Pyrotechnical compounds;
        Priming explosives:
            Fulminate of mercury;
            Nitride of lead;
            Trinitroresorcinate of lead;
            Tetrazene;
        Chlorated explosives;
        Nitrate explosives with dinitrotoluene, or with dinitronaphthalene;
        Hydrogen peroxide at less than 60%;
        Nitrocelluloses;
        Black powder;
        Nitric acid at less than 99%;
        Hydrate of hydogine at less than 30%.
4. *Armoured equipment.*
    a. Tanks
    b. Armoured vehicles.
    c. Armoured trains.
5. *Warships of all types.*
6. *Military aircraft of all types.*
7. *Atomic weapons.*
8. *Biological weapons* (1).   ⎰ According to definitions
9. *Chemical weapons* (1).   ⎱   given in Annex II, hereinbelow
  10. Constituent parts which can be used only in the construction of one of the items enumerated in groups 1, 2, 4, 5, and 6 hereinabove (2).
  11. Machines which can be used only for the manufacture of one of the items enumerated in groups 1, 2, 4, 5, and 6 hereinabove (2).

(1) The Commissariat may exempt from the requirement of authorisation chemical and biological substances the use of which is primarily civilian. If the Commissariat decides that it is unable to grant such exemptions, it shall limit the control which it exercises solely to the use of such substances.

(2) The production of models of, and the technical research concerning, the materials defined in paragraphs 10 and 11 hereinabove are not subject to the appropriate provisions of Article 107.

Annex II to Article 107

The present annex shall be deemed to include the weapons defined in Paragraphs I–VI and the manufacturing facilities especially designed for their production. Nevertheless, the provisions of Paragraphs II–VI of this annex shall be deemed to exclude any device or assembly, apparatus, production facilities, product and agency utilised for civilian purposes or serving research for scientific, medical and industrial purposes in the spheres of pure and applied science.

    I.   *Atomic Weapons.*

        a.   An atomic weapon is defined as any weapon which contains, or is designed to contain or utilise, nuclear fuel or radioactive isotopes and which, by explosion or other uncontrolled nuclear transformation of the nuclear fuel, or by radioactivity of the nuclear fuel or radioactive isotopes, is capable of mass destruction, mass injury or mass poisoning.

        b.   Furthermore, any part, device, assembly or material especially designed for, or primarily useful in, any weapon as set forth under Paragraph *a*, shall be deemed to be an atomic weapon.

        c.   Any quantity of nuclear fuel produced in any one year in excess of 500 grammes will be considered material especially designed for, or primarily useful in, atomic weapons.

        d.   Nuclear fuel as used in the preceding definition includes plutonium, Uranium 233, Uranium 235 (including Uranium 235 contained in Uranium enriched to over 2.I per cent by weight of Uranium 235) and any other material capable of releasing substantial quantities of atomic energy through nuclear fission or fusion or other nuclear reaction of the material. The foregoing materials shall be considered to be nuclear fuel regardless of the chemical or physical form in which they exist.

    II.   *Chemical Weapons.*

        a.   A chemical weapon is defined as any equipment or apparatus expressly designed to use, for military purposes, the asphyxiating, toxic, irritant, paralysant, growth-regulating, anti-lubricating or catalysing properties of any chemical substance.

        b.   Subject to the provisions of Paragraph *c*, chemical substances, having such properties and capable of being used in the equipment or apparatus referred to in Paragraph *a*, shall be deemed to be included in this definition.

        c.   Such apparatus and such quantities of the chemical substances as are referred to in Paragraphs *a* and *b* which do not exceed peaceful civilian requirements shall be deemed to be excluded from this definition.

    III.   *Biological Weapons.*

        a.   A biological weapon is defined as any equipment or apparatus expressly designed to use, for military purposes, harmful insects or other living or dead organisms, or their toxic products.

        b.   Subject to the provisions of Paragraph *c*, insects, organisms and their toxic products of such nature and in such amounts as to make them capable of being used in the equipment or apparatus referred to in *a* shall be deemed to be included in this definition.

        c.   Such equipment or apparatus and such quantities of the insects, organisms and their toxic products as are referred to in Paragraphs *a* and *b* which do not exceed peaceful civilian requirements shall be deemed to be excluded from the definition of biological weapons.

    IV.   *Long-range Missiles, Guided Missiles and Influence Mines.*

        a.   Subject to the provisions of Paragraph *d*, long range missiles and guided missiles are defined as missiles such that the velocity or direction of motion can be influenced after the instant of launching by a device or mechanism inside or outside the missile, including V-type weapons developed in the recent war and subsequent modifications thereof. Combustion is considered as a mechanism which may influence the velocity.

b. Subject to the provisions of Paragraph *d*, influence mines are defined as naval mines which can be exploded automatically by influences which emanate solely from external sources, including influence mines developed in the recent war and subsequent modifications thereof.

c. Parts, devices or assemblies specially designed for use in or with the weapons referred to in Paragraphs *a* and *b* shall be deemed to be included in this definition.

d. Proximity fuses, and short-range guided missiles for anti-aircraft defence with the following maximum characteristics, are regarded as excluded from this definition:
Length, 2 metres;
Diameter, 30 centimetres;
Velocity, 660 metres per second:
Ground range, 32 kilometres;
Weight of war-head, 22.5 kilograms.

V. *Naval Vessels other than Minor Defensive Craft.*
Naval vessels other than minor defensive craft mean:
a. Warships over 1,500 tons displacement.
b. Submarines.
c. All warships powered by means other than steam, diesel or petrol engines or gas turbines or jets.

VI. *Military Aircraft.*
Complete military aircraft and components thereof, as listed below:-
a. Air frames–centre section spars, wing panel spars, longerons.
b. Jet engines–centrifugal impellors, turbo discs, burners, axial flow centre shafts.
c. Reciprocating engines–cylinder blocks, supercharger impellors.

Article 107 bis

The regulations provided for in Paragraph 3 of Article 107 hereinabove shall be submitted to the Council within three months after entry into effect of the Treaty. In the interim, the Commissariat shall grant authorisations in appropriate cases.

Article 108

1. Without prejudice to the provisions of Article 114 hereinbelow the Commissariat may, as concerns the war materials defined in the Annexes to Article 107, address itself directly to the enterprises in question for information necessary to the fulfillment of its mission; the interested governments shall be kept informed.

The Commissariat may cause its agents to proceed to necessary verifications.

2. At the request of the Commissariat, the Court may, under the conditions set forth in the Jurisdictional Statute referred to in Article 67, impose fines on such firms as disregard obligations devolving on them through decisions taken in application of the provisions of the present Article, or which knowingly furnish false information. Such fines shall not exceed a maximum of 1% of the annual turnover, and the daily fines for delayed execution shall not exceed a maximum of 5% of the average daily turnover for each day of delay.

Article 109

In order to aid the Commissariat in the performance of the tasks provided for in Articles 101 and 102 hereinabove a Consultative Committee shall be established. It shall be composed of at least 20 and, at the most, 34 members. It shall include, specifically, representatives of producers and of labour; the numbers of the producers' representatives and of the representatives of labour shall be equal.

The Committee shall include nationals of each of the member States.

The members of the Consultative Committee shall be appointed by the Council, acting by a two-thirds majority. They shall be designated in their personal capacities for a term of two years. No order or instruction from organisations which have nominated them shall be binding on them.

its executive bureau, for a period of one year. The Committee shall draw up its own internal regulations.

The compensation allowed members of the Consultative Committee shall be set by the Council on the proposal of the Commissariat.

Article 110

The Consultative Committee shall be consulted by the Commissariat concerning problems of an economic and social nature raised by the preparation or execution of the common armament, equipment, supply and infrastructure programmes. The Commissariat shall submit to the Consultative Committee any information needed in the latter's deliberations.

The Consultative Committee shall be convened by its President upon the request of the Commissariat.

Minutes of the discussions of the Consultative Committee shall be transmitted to the Commissariat and the Council at the same time as are the Committee's recommendations.

Article 111

In consultation with the governments of the member States, the Commissariat shall prepare plans for the mobilisation of the economic resources of the member States.

Title VI
General Provisions

Article 112

The member States undertake to take all general or specific measures appropriate to ensure the carrying out of obligations imposed by decisions and recommendations of institutions of the Community; they undertake also to facilitate the accomplishment by the Community of its mission.

The member States undertake to refrain from acts incompatible with the provisions of the present Treaty.

Article 113

All the institutions and services of the Community and of the member States shall collaborate closely concerning questions of common interest.

They shall lend each other mutual aid in administrative and legal matters in accordance with agreements to be entered into among themselves.

Article 114

1. The member States undertake to place at the disposal of the Commissariat all information necessary for the accomplishment of its mission. The Commissariat may request the member States to cause necessary verifications to be made. Upon the request of the Commissariat, which shall be supported by a statement of reasons, its agents shall be permitted to participate in making these verifications.

The Council, by a two-thirds vote, may give general directives concerning the application of the preceding Subparagraph.

If a member State believes that the information requested from it by the Commissariat is not needed for the accomplishment of the latter's mission, it may, within ten days, request a ruling from the Court. The Court shall rule as a matter of urgency. While such a request is pending, the information in question need not be made available.

2. The institutions of the Community, their staffs and their agents shall not divulge information which is in the nature of a professional or a military secret.

Any violation of such secrets may, if damage has resulted therefrom, be the basis for a damage suit in the Court.

Article 115

Within the limits of its competence, agents of the Commissariat charged by it with supervisory missions shall enjoy, as against individuals or public or private enterprises on the territories of member States, to the extent necessary for the accomplishment of their mission, such rights and powers as are granted by the laws of such States to agents of comparable departments of their own governments. Missions and the status of the agents charged with such missions shall be duly communicated to the State in question.

Officials of such State may, at the request of such State, or of the Commissariat, assist agents of the Commissariat in carrying out their verification operations.

Articles 116

Under the terms of an agreement to be entered into by the member States, the Community shall enjoy on the territories of the member States the privileges and immunities necessary to the accomplishment of its mission.

Article 117

If the Commissariat determines that a member State has failed to carry out an obligation imposed upon it by the present Treaty, it shall so inform that State and invite its comments; such comments shall be submitted within a period of one month.

If at the expiration of an additional one-month period there persists a difference of opinion between the Commissariat and the State concerned, either may have recourse to the the Court. The latter shall decide the case as a matter of urgency.

The Council shall be informed of the decision of the Court.

Article 118

The seat of the institutions of the Community shall be determined by agreement among the member States.

Article 119

Without prejudice to the provisions of Title V of the Military Protocol, the languages to be employed by the institutions of the Community shall be determined by unanimous decision of the Council.

Article 120

1. The present Treaty is applicable to the European territories of the member States.

2. By decision of the Commissariat taken with the unanimous concurrence of the Council:

a. elements of the European Defence Forces may, with the agreement of the competent Supreme Commander responsible to the North Atlantic Treaty Organisation, be stationed in territories, other than those defined in Paragraph 1 of this Article, which are included in the area defined in Article 6 of the North Atlantic Treaty.

b. schools, training centres and other establishments of the Community may be installed in territories, other than those defined in Paragraph 1 of this Article, which are included in the area defined in Subparagraph *a* of the Paragraph, as well as in Africa north of the Tropic of Cancer.

3. By virtue of a unanimous decision to this effect taken by the Council after parliamentary approval, if and as required by the constitutional rules of each member State:

— Elements of the European Defence Forces may be stationed in territories other than those defined in Sections 1, 2, *a* of this Article;

— Schools, training centres and other establishments of the Community may be installed in territories other than those defined in Paragraph 1 and Paragraph 2, Subparagraph *b*.

This decision of the Council shall be taken after consultation with the North Atlantic Council and with the agreement of the competent Supreme Commander responsible to the North Atlantic Treaty Organisation.

4. Member States are authorised to recruit for the needs of contingents furnished by them to the European Defence Forces in territories other than those defined in Paragraph 1 of this Article which are subject to their jurisdiction or for which they assume international responsibility.

Article 121

The member States undertake not to enter into any international agreement incompatible with the present Treaty.

Article 122

The member States undertake not to permit any treaties, conventions or declarations existing among themselves, with a view to settling differences concerning the interpretation or application of the present Treaty by means or a procedure other than that provided by the present Treaty, to prevail over the present Treaty.

Article 123

1. In case of serious and urgent necessity, the Council shall assume, or confer upon institutions of the Community of other appropriate organisations, such powers as are necessary to meet the situation, within the limits of the general mission of the Community and with a view to ensuring the achievement of its objectives; this decision shall be taken by unanimous vote.

A serious and urgent necessity may result either from the situations referred to in Paragraph 3, Article 2 of the present Treaty, or in the Treaty between the member States and the U.K. of the same date, or in the Additional Protocol concerning Guarantees between the European Defence Community and the North Atlantic Treaty Organisation, or from a declaration to that effect adopted by unanimous vote of the Council.

2.   The provisional measures taken pursuant to Paragraph 1 of this Article shall cease to be effective on the date on which the state of emergency is declared by the Council, by two-thirds vote, to be at an end.

The normally competent institutions shall, in the manner provided for in this Treaty, decide concerning the maintenance of conditions resulting from these measures.

3.   The present Article does not affect the placing in action of the European Defence Forces for the purpose of meeting an aggression.

Article 124

In any case not provided for in the present Treaty in which a decision or recommendation of the Commissariat appears necessary to ensure the proper functioning of the Community and the attainment of its objective within the limits of its general mission, such decision or recommendation may be taken with the unanimous concurrence of the Council.

If the Commissariat fails to take the initiative, the matter may be referred to the Council by one of the member States. The Council may, by unanimous vote, require the Commissariat to make such decision or recommendation. If the Commissariat fails to take action pursuant to such decision of the Council within the time limit set therein, the Council shall be empowered to take such measures itself by a simple majority.

Article 125

If unforeseen difficulties which are brought out by experience in the application of the present Treaty require an adjustment of the rules concerning the exercise by the Commissariat of the powers which are conferred upon it, appropriate modifications may be made in such powers by unanimous decision of the Council provided that such modifications do not bring into question the provisions of Article 2 hereinabove or modify the relationship among the powers of the Commissariat and of the other institutions of the Community.

Article 126

The Government of each member State and the Commissariat may propose amendments to the present Treaty. Such proposals shall be submitted to the Council. If the Council, acting by a two-thirds majority, approves a conference of representatives of the Governments of the member States, such a conference shall be immediately convened by the President of the Council, with a view to agreeing to any modifications to be made in the provisions of the Treaty.

Such amendments shall enter into force after having been ratified by all the member States in conformity with their respective constitutional processes.

Article 127

As used in the present Treaty, the words 'The present Treaty' shall mean the provisions of this Treaty and those of:

1.   the Military Protocol;
2.   the Jurisdictional Protocol;
3.   the Military Penal Law Protocol;
4.   the Financial Protocol;
5.   the Protocol concerning the Remuneration of Civilian and Military Personnel of the Community and their Pension Rights;
6.   the Protocol concerning the Grand Duchy of Luxembourg;

7. the Protocol concerning Relations between the European Defence Community and the North Atlantic Treaty Organisation;

8. the Protocol concerning Mutual Assistance Guarantees between the European Defence Community and the North Atlantic Treaty Organisation.

Article 128

The present Treaty is concluded for a period of 50 years from the date of its entry into effect.

If, before the establishment of a European federation or confederation, the North Atlantic Treaty should cease to be in effect or there should be an essential modification in the membership of the North Atlantic Treaty Organisation, the High Contracting Parties shall examine together the new situation which shall thus have arisen.

Article 129

Any European State may request to accede to the present Treaty. The Council, after having obtained the opinion of the Commissariat, shall act by unanimous vote, and shall also fix the terms of accession by unanimous vote. Accession shall become effective on the day on which the instrument of accession is received by the Government acting as depository of the Treaty.

Article 130

The present Treaty, drawn up in a single original, shall be deposited in the archives of the government of the French Republic, which shall transmit a certified true copy to each of the governments of the other signatory States.

As soon as it shall have assumed its function, the Council shall establish authentic texts of the present Treaty in the languages other than that of the original. In the case of discrepancies, the text of the original shall govern.

Article 131

The present Treaty shall be ratified and its provisions applied in accordance with the constitutional rules of each member State. The instruments of ratification shall be deposited in the archives of the Government of the French Republic, which shall notify the Governments of the other member States when the instruments have been so deposited.

Article 132

The present Treaty shall enter into effect on the date of the deposit of the instrument of ratification of the last signatory nation to accomplish that formality.

In the event that all the instruments of ratification have not been deposited within a period of six months following the signature of the present Treaty, the governments of the States which have made such deposit shall consult among themselves on the measures to be taken.

IN WITNESS WHEREOF the undersigned Plenipotentiaries have affixed their signatures at the end of the present Treaty and have thereto affixed their seals.

DONE in Paris the twenty-seventh day of May one thousand nine hundred fifty-two.

Konrad Adenauer   Robert Schuman   Joseph Bech
Paul Van Zeeland   Alcide de Gasperi   Dirk Stikker

PROTOCOL CONCERNING RELATIONS BETWEEN THE EUROPEAN DEFENCE COMMUNITY AND THE NORTH ATLANTIC TREATY ORGANISATION

The member States of the European Defence Community,
Desirous that relations between the North Atlantic Treaty Organisation and the European Defence Community maintain the greatest flexibility and avoid to the greatest extent possible the overlapping of responsibilities and functions,
Agree as follows:

1. *Mutual consultations shall take place between the North Atlantic Council and the Council of the European Defence Community on questions concerning the common objectives of the two organisations, and the two Councils shall hold joint meetings whenever one or the other deems it desirable.*

Whenever one of the parties to the North Atlantic Treaty or one of the parties to the Treaty establishing the European Defence Community shall consider that the territorial integrity, the political independence or the security of one of them is threatened, or that the existence or the integrity of the North Atlantic Treaty Organisation or of the European Defence Community is threatened, a joint meeting shall be held upon the request of such party in order to study measures to be taken to deal with the situation.

2. With a view to ensuring close coordination on the technical level, each Organisation shall communicate to the other appropriate information, and a *permanent contact shall be established between the staffs of the Commissariat of the European Defence Community and of the civilian agencies of the North Atlantic Treaty Organisation.*

3. As soon as the European Defence Forces shall have been placed under the command of a Commander responsible to the North Atlantic Treaty Organisation, members of the European Defence Forces shall become members of such Commander's Headquarters and appropriate subordinate Headquarters. Commanders responsible to the North Atlantic Treaty Organisation shall ensure all necessary liaison between the European Defence Forces and the other military agencies of the North Atlantic Treaty Organisation.

4. The Council of the European Defence Community and the North Atlantic Council may, by common agreement, adjust the foregoing arrangement governing relationships defined hereinabove.

5. The present Protocol shall enter into effect at the same time as the Treaty establishing the European Defence Community, of which it shall form an integral part.

DONE in Paris the twenty-seventh day of May one thousand nine hundred fifty-two.

Konrad Adenauer
Paul Van Zeeland
Robert Schuman
Alcide de Gasperi
Joseph Bech
Dirk Stikker

PROTOCOL CONCERNING GUARANTEES OF ASSISTANCE FROM THE MEMBER STATES OF THE COMMUNITY TO THE STATES PARTIES TO THE NORTH ATLANTIC TREATY

The member States of the European Defence Community,
Convinced that the creation of the European Defence Community, established by the Treaty signed in Paris on May 27, 1952, will strengthen the North Atlantic Community and the common defence of the North Atlantic area, and will promote a closer association of the countries of Western Europe,
Agree as follows:

Article 1

Any armed attack:
(i) on the territory of one or more of the Parties to the North Atlantic Treaty in the area defined in Article 6 (i) of the said Treaty;
(ii) on the land, naval or air forces of any of the Parties to the North Atlantic Treaty when in the area described in Article 6 (ii) of that Treaty, will be considered as an armed attack against the member States of the European Defence Community and against the European Defence Forces.

In the event of such an armed attack, the member States of the European Defence Community, in respect of themselves and of the European Defence Forces, shall have the same obligations towards the Parties to the North Atlantic Treaty as those Parties undertake towards the members of the European Defence Community and the European Defence Forces, by virtue of the Protocol between the parties to the North Atlantic Treaty referred to in Article 2 hereinafter.

The expression 'States Parties to the North Atlantic Treaty' shall mean parties to the said Treaty at the time of entry into effect of the present Protocol.

Article 2

The present Protocol shall enter into effect at the same time as the Protocol signed among the States Parties to the North Atlantic Treaty, which extends reciprocal guarantees to the member States of the European Defence Community and to the European Defence Forces.

Article 3

The present Protocol shall remain in effect for so long as the Treaty establishing the European Defence Community, and the North Atlantic Treaty remain in effect, and the States Parties to this latter Treaty shall continue to grant, insofar as they and their forces are concerned, guarantees to the member States of the European Defence Community and to the European Defence Forces which are equivalent to the guarantees set forth in this Protocol.

Article 4

The present Protocol will be deposited in the archives of the French Republic, which will transmit certified copies to the governments of all the States who are Parties to the Treaty creating the European Defence Community and of all the States who are Parties to the North Atlantic Treaty.

DONE in Paris the twenty-seventh day of May one thousand nine hundred fifty-two.

> Konrad Adenauer
> Paul Van Zeeland
> Robert Schuman
> Alcide de Gasperi
> Joseph Bech
> Dirk Stikker

TREATY BETWEEN THE UNITED KINGDOM AND THE MEMBER STATES OF THE EUROPEAN DEFENCE COMMUNITY

The President of the Federal Republic of Germany, His Majesty the King of the Belgians, the President of the French Republic, the President of the Italian Republic, Her Royal Highness the Grand Duchess of Luxembourg, Her Majesty the Queen of the Netherlands and Her Majesty the Queen of Great Britain, Ireland and the British Dominions beyond the Seas,

Desiring in the interests of the defence of Western Europe to extend, as between the United Kingdom and the States members of the European Defence Community established by the Treaty and signed in Paris on the 27th day of May 1952, the guarantees of assistance against aggression given in Article (6) of the Treaty signed at Brussels on the 17th of March 1948,

Having appointed as their plenipotentiaries for this purpose,

The President of the Federal Republic of Germany,

Dr. Konrad Adenauer, Chancellor, Minister of Foreign Affairs;

His Majesty the King of the Belgians,

Mr. Paul Van Zeeland, Minister of Foreign Affairs;

The President of the French Republic,

Mr. Robert Schuman, Minister of Foreign Affairs;

The President of the Italian Republic,

Mr. De Gasperi, Minister of Foreign Affairs;

Her Royal Highness the Grand Duchess of Luxembourg,

Mr. Bech, Minister of Foreign Affairs;

Her Majesty the Queen of the Netherlands,

Mr. Stikker, Minister of Foreign Affairs;

Her Majesty the Queen of Great Britain, Ireland and the British Dominions beyond the Seas,

Mr. Anthony Eden, Foreign Secretary.
Who, having exhibited their full powers found in good and due form, have agreed as follows:

Article 1

If at any time, while the United Kingdom is Party to the North Atlantic Treaty, any other Party to the present Treaty which is at that time a member of the European Defence Community, or the European Defence Forces, should be the object of an armed attack in Europe, the United Kingdom will, in accordance with Article 51 of the United National Charter, afford the Party or the Forces so attacked all the military and other aid and assistance in its power.

Article 2

If at any time while Article 1 remains in force the United Kingdom or its armed forces should be the object of an armed attack in Europe, the other Parties to the present Treaty which are at that time members of the European Defence Community, and the European Defence Forces, will afford the United Kingdom and its forces all the military and other aid and assistance in their power.

Article 3

The present Treaty shall be ratified and its provisions carried out by the signatories in accordance with their respective constitutional processes. The instruments of ratification shall be deposited with the Government of the United Kingdom, which shall notify the Governments of the other signatories of each deposit. The Treaty shall enter into force when all the signatories have deposited their instruments of ratification and the Council of the European Defence Community has notified the Government of the United Kingdom that the Treaty establishing the European Defence Community has entered into force.

Article 4

The present Treaty, of which the English and French texts are equally authentic, shall be deposited in the archives of the Government of the United Kingdom which shall transmit a certified copy thereof to the Government of each of the other signatories.

In witness whereof the undersigned plenipotentiaries have signed the present Treaty and have affixed thereto their seals.

DONE in Paris, the twenty-seventh day of May, one thousand nine hundred fifty-two.

Konrad Adenauer
Paul Van Zeeland
Robert Schuman
Alcide de Gasperi
Joseph Bech
Dirk Stikker
Anthony Eden

PROTOCOL TO THE NORTH ATLANTIC TREATY ON GUARANTEES GIVEN BY THE PARTIES TO THE NORTH ATLANTIC TREATY TO THE MEMBERS OF THE EUROPEAN DEFENCE COMMUNITY

The parties to the North Atlantic Treaty, signed at Washington on 4th April 1949,

Being satisfied that the creation of the European Defence Community set up under the Treaty signed at Paris on 27th May 1952 will strengthen the North Atlantic Community and the integrated defence of the North Atlantic area, and promote the closer association of the countries of Western Europe, and,

Considering that the Parties to the Treaty setting up the European Defence Community have signed a Protocol, which will enter into force at the same time as the present Protocol, giving to the Parties to the North Atlantic Treaty guarantees equivalent to the guarantees contained in Article 5 of the North Atlantic Treaty,

Agree as follows:

Article 1

An armed attack

1. on the territory of any of the members of the European Defence Community in Europe or in the area described in Article 6 (i) of the North Atlantic Treaty, or

2. on the forces, vessels or aircraft of the European Defence Community when in the area described in Article 6 (ii) of the said Treaty, shall be considered an attack against all the Parties to the North Atlantic Treaty, within the meaning of Article 5 of the said Treaty, and Article 5 shall apply accordingly.

The expression 'member of the European Defence Community' in Paragraph 1 of this Article means any of the following States which is a member of the Community, namely, Belgium, France, the German Federal Republic, Italy, Luxembourg, and the Netherlands.

Article 2

The present Protocol shall enter into force as soon as each of the Parties has notified the Government of the United States of America of its acceptance and the Council of the European Defence Community has notified the North Atlantic Council of the entry into force of the Treaty setting up the European Defence Community. The Government of the United States of America shall inform all the Parties to the North Atlantic Treaty of the date of the receipt of each such notification and of the date of entry into force of the present Protocol.

Article 3

The present Protocol shall remain in force for so long as the North Atlantic Treaty and the Treaty setting up the European Defence Community remain in force and the Parties to the latter Treaty continue to give in respect of themselves and the European Defence Forces guarantees to the Parties to the North Atlantic Treaty equivalent to the guarantees contained in the present Protocol.

Article 4

The present Protocol, of which the English and French texts are equally authentic, shall be deposited in the Archives of the Government of the United States of America. Duly certified copies thereof shall be transmitted by that Government to the Governments of all the Parties to the North Atlantic Treaty and of all the Parties to the Treaty setting up the European Defence Community.

In witness whereof, the undersigned plenipotentiaries have signed the present Protocol.

DONE in Paris the twenty-seventh day of May, one thousand nine hundred fifty two.

For the Kingdom of Belgium: Van Zeeland.
For Canada: Heeney.
For the Kingdom of Denmark: Steense-Leth.
For France: Schuman.
For the Kingdom of Greece: Pipinelis.
For Iceland: Petursson.
For Italy: De Gasperi.
For the Grand Duchy of Luxembourg: Bech.
For the Kingdom of the Netherlands: Stikker.
For the Kingdom of Norway: Skaug.
For Portugal: De Tovar.
For Turkey: Ali Tiney.
For the United Kingdom of Great Britain and Northern Ireland: Eden.
For the United States of America: Acheson.

TRIPARTITE DECLARATION

The Governments of France, the United Kingdom of Great Britain and Northern Ireland, and the United States of America have signed conventions with the German Federal Republic which will establish a new relationship with that country. These conventions, as well as the treaties for a European Defence Community and a European Coal and Steel Community, of which France is a signatory, provide a new basis for uniting Europe and for the realisation of Germany's partnership in the European Community. They are designed to prevent the resurgence of former tensions and conflicts among the free nations of Europe and any future revival of aggressive militarism. They make possible the removal of the special restraints hitherto imposed on the Federal Republic of Germany and permit its participation as an equal partner in Western Defence.

These conventions and treaties respond to the desire to provide by united efforts for the prosperity and security of Western Europe. The Governments of the United Kingdom and the United States consider that the establishment and development of these institutions of the European Community correspond to their own basic interests and will therefore lend them every possible cooperation and support.

Moreover, Western Defence is a common enterprise in which the Governments of the United Kingdom and the United States are already partners through membership of the North Atlantic Treaty Organisation.

These bonds are now strengthened by the system of reciprocal guarantees agreed to between the member States of the European Defence Community, between these member States and the United Kingdom and also between these member States and the member States of the North Atlantic Treaty Organisation.

For these various reasons, including the fact that these new guarantees will apply to the States concerned only as members of one or the other of these organisations, the Governments of the United Kingdom and the United States have an abiding interest, as has the Government of France, in the effectiveness of the Treaty creating the European Defence Community and in the strength and integrity of that Community. Accordingly, if any action from whatever quarter threatens the integrity or unity of the Community, the two Governments will regard this as a threat to their own security. They will act in accordance with Article 4 of the North Atlantic Treaty. Moreover, they have each expressed their resolve to station such forces on the continent of Europe, including the Federal Republic of Germany, as they deem necessary and appropriate to contribute to the joint defence of the North Atlantic Treaty area, having regard to their obligations under the North Atlantic Treaty, their interest in the integrity of the European Defence Community, and their special responsibilities in Germany.

The security and welfare of Berlin and the maintenance of the position of the three powers there are regarded by the three powers as essential elements of the peace of the free world in the present international situation. Accordingly, they will maintain armed forces within the territory of Berlin as long as their responsibilities require it. They therefore reaffirm that they will treat any attack against Berlin from any quarter as an attack upon their forces and themselves.

These new security guarantees supersede the assurances contained in the declaration of the Foreign Ministers of France, the United Kingdom and the United States at New York on September 19th, 1950.

Dean Acheson
Robert Schuman
Anthony Eden

Paris, May 27th, 1952.

The North Atlantic Treaty

Washington DC, 4 April 1949[1]

The Parties to this Treaty reaffirm their faith in the purposes and principles of the Charter of the United Nations and their desire to live in peace with all peoples and all governments.

They are determined to safeguard the freedom, common heritage and civilisation of their peoples, founded on the principles of democracy, individual liberty and the rule of law.

They seek to promote stability and well-being in the North Atlantic area.

They are resolved to unite their efforts for collective defence and for the preservation of peace and security.

They therefore agree to this North Atlantic Treaty:

Article 1

The Parties undertake, as set forth in the Charter of the United Nations, to settle any international dispute in which they may be involved by peaceful means in such a manner that international peace and security and justice are not endangered, and to refrain in their international relations from the threat or use of force in any manner inconsistent with the purposes of the United Nations.

---

[1] The Treaty came into force on 24 August 1949, after the deposition of the ratifications of all signatory states.

Article 2

The Parties will contribute toward the further development of peaceful and friendly international relations by strengthening their free institutions, by bringing about a better understanding of the principles upon which these institutions are founded, and by promoting conditions of stability and well-being. They will seek to eliminate conflict in their international economic policies and will encourage economic collaboration between any or all of them.

Article 3

In order more effectively to achieve the objectives of this Treaty, the Parties, separately and jointly, by means of continuous and effective self-help and mutual aid, will maintain and develop their individual and collective capacity to resist armed attack.

Article 4

The Parties will consult together whenever, in the opinion of any of them, the territorial integrity, political independence or security of any of the Parties is threatened.

Article 5

The Parties agree that an armed attack against one or more of them in Europe or North America shall be considered an attack against them all, and consequently they agree that, if such an armed attack occurs, each of them, in exercise of the right of individual or collective self-defence recognised by Article 51 of the Charter of the United Nations, will assist the Party or Parties so attacked by taking forthwith, individually, and in concert with the other Parties, such action as it deems necessary, including the use of armed force, to restore and maintain the security of the North Atlantic area.

Any such armed attack and all measures taken as a result thereof shall immediately be reported to the Security Council. Such measures shall be terminated when the Security Council has taken the measures necessary to restore and maintain international peace and security.

Article 6[1]

For the purpose of Article 5, an armed attack on one or more of the

Parties is deemed to include an armed attack:
— on the territory of any of the Parties in Europe or North America, on the Algerian Departments of France[2], on the territory of Turkey or on the islands under the jurisdiction of any of the Parties in the North Atlantic area north of the Tropic of Cancer;
— on the forces, vessels, or aircraft of any of the Parties, when in or over these territories or any other area in Europe in which occupation forces of any of the Parties were stationed on the date when the Treaty entered into force or the Mediterranean Sea or the North Atlantic area north of the Tropic of Cancer.

Article 7

The Treaty does not affect, and shall not be interpreted as affecting, in any way the rights and obligations under the Charter of the Parties which are members of the United Nations, or the primary responsibility of the Security Council for the maintenance of international peace and security.

Article 8

Each Party declares that none of the international engagements now in force between it and any other of the Parties or any third State is in conflict with the provisions of this Treaty, and undertakes not to enter into any international engagement in conflict with this Treaty.

Article 9

The Parties hereby establish a Council, on which each of them shall be represented, to consider matters concerning the implementation of this Treaty. The Council shall be so organised as to be able to meet promptly at any time. The Council shall set up such subsidiary bodies as may be necessary; in particular it shall establish immediately a defence committee which shall recommend measures for the implementation of Articles 3 and 5.

[1] As amended by Article 2 of the Protocol to the North Atlantic Treaty on the accession of Greece and Turkey, signed on 22 October, 1951.
[2] On 16 January 1963 the Council noted that in so far as the former Algerian Departments of France were concerned, the relevant clauses of this Treaty had become inapplicable as from 3rd July 1962.

Article 10

The Parties may, by unanimous agreement, invite any other European State in a position to further the principles of this Treaty and to contribute to the security of the North Atlantic area to accede to this Treaty. Any State so invited may become a party to the Treaty by depositing its instrument of accession with the Government of the United States of America. The Government of the United States of America will inform each of the Parties of the deposit of each such instrument of accession.

Article 11

This Treaty shall be ratified and its provisions carried out by the Parties in accordance with their respective constitutional processes. The instruments of ratification shall be deposited as soon as possible with the Government of the United States of America, which will notify all the other signatories of each deposit. The Treaty shall enter into force between the States which have ratified it as soon as the ratifications of the majority of the signatories, including the ratifications of Belgium, Canada, France, Luxembourg, the Netherlands, the United Kingdom and the United States, have been deposited and shall come into effect with respect to other States on the date of the deposit of their ratifications.

Article 12

After the Treaty has been in force for ten years, or at any time thereafter, the Parties shall, if any of them so requests, consult together for the purpose of reviewing the Treaty, having regard for the factors then affecting peace and security in the North Atlantic area including the development of universal as well as regional arrangements under the Charter of the United Nations for the maintenance of international peace and security.

Article 13

After the Treaty has been in force for twenty years, any Party may cease to be a Party one year after its notice of denunciation has been given to the Government of the United States of America, which will inform the Governments of the other Parties of the deposit of each notice of denunciation.

Article 14

This Treaty, of which the English and French texts are equally authentic, shall be deposited in the archives of the Government of the United States of America. Duly certified copies will be transmitted by that Government to the Governments of the other signatories.

AGREED INTERPRETATIONS OF THE NORTH ATLANTIC TREATY*

During the exploratory talks which resulted in the draft Treaty, agreement was reached on the meaning of certain phrases and articles. These agreements were not formal, but constituted the understanding of the representatives participating in the discussions as to the interpretation of those phrases and articles. The committee reviewed those interpretations and instructed the Secretary to make note of them. They are:

'(1) The participation of Italy in the North Atlantic Treaty has no effect upon the provisions of the Italian Peace Treaty.

'(2) 'Mutual aid' under Article 3 means the contribution by each Party, consistent with its geographic location and resources and with due regard to the requirements of economic recovery, of such mutual aid as it can reasonably be expected to contribute in the form in which it can most effectively furnish it, e.g. facilities, manpower, productive capacity, or military equipment.

'(3) Article 4 is applicable in the event of a threat in any part of the world, to the security of any of the Parties, including a threat to the security of their overseas territories.

'(4) a. For the purposes of Article 6 the British and American forces in the Free Territory of Trieste are understood to be occupation forces.

'b. The words 'North Atlantic area north of the Tropic of Cancer' in Article 6 mean the general area of the North Atlantic Ocean north

* *Foreign Relations of the United States, 1949*, Volume IV, pages 222–223. Minutes of the Ambassadors' Committee, March 15, 1949.

of that line, including adjacent sea and air spaces between the territories covered by that Article.

'(5) With reference to Article 8, it is understood that no previous international engagements to which any of the participating states are parties would in any way interfere with the carrying out of their obligations under this Treaty.

'(6) The Council, as Article 9 specifically states, is established 'to consider matters concerning the implementation of the Treaty' and is empowered 'to set up such subsidiary bodies as may be necessary'. This is a broad rather than specific definition of functions and is not intended to exclude the performance at appropriate levels in the organisation of such planning for the implementation of Articles 3 and 5 or other functions as the Parties may agree to be necessary.

'(7) It is the common understanding that the primary purpose of this Treaty is to provide for the collective self-defence of the Parties, as countries having common interests in the North Atlantic area, while reaffirming their existing obligations for the maintenance of peace and the settlement of disputes between them.

'It is further understood that the Parties will, in their public statements, stress this primary purpose, recognised and preserved by Article 5I, rather than any specific connection with Chapter VIII or other Articles of the United Nations Charter.'

APPENDIX IV

The Atlantic Alliance
and German Unity

Text of an address given by the Secretary General of NATO,
Mr Manfred Wörner, in Hamburg on 8 February 1990

The question of European security is one that must now be looked at afresh. The rigid military confrontation of past decades is increasingly giving way to a concern for enhanced security and to the active pursuit of peace using a combination of military and political elements. Two tasks have to be faced in the coming years:

● the development of a new security structure, and
● the creation of a new political order in Europe.

Both tasks are equally indispensable for the preservation and strengthening of peace in the long run.

The Alliance therefore faces a dual challenge. It must be a driving and guiding force in the dynamic process of change from the *status quo*, helping to establish a new continental order of peace and freedom. In the second place, it must be a source of stability, guaranteeing security in Europe, especially in the face of erratic developments in the Soviet Union and a difficult transitional period in Central and Eastern Europe.

The task of working out a new European security equation for the 21st century offers a historic opportunity. Under pressure for comprehensive change in its system the Soviet Union favours a new security

127

order. The basic premises of Western security and stability — the presence of United States troops on the European continent, the continuation of the Atlantic Alliance and an ultimate nuclear deterrent to uphold peace — are today increasingly acknowledged by the Soviet Union as being prerequisites for stability and fundamentals of a future security structure.

I believe the following points to be important:

● Only the transatlantic link, the continued integration of America in our security structures, can guarantee stability in the long term. The United States commitment to European security is the cornerstone of the Western system that was created after the Second World War, and which has given us peace. Without the active participation of North America it will not be possible to balance the Germans' interest in unity, their neighbours' concerns and the Soviet Union's legitimate security interests, and to reach a common position.

● The Alliance, which is the concrete expression of this transatlantic link, remains indispensable for a future security scheme. At the same time, the Alliance will still have the function of guiding the ongoing arms control process.

● The starting point for the future European security structure is provided by the Vienna negotiations. Initial results must lead to yet further reductions in force levels and new defensive structures. The latest United States proposal to reduce American and Soviet troops in Central Europe to less than 200,000 shows the way. Future conventional disarmament in Europe must not remain a matter of mere bean-counting, however. It must not merely cover force levels, but also build-up capability, logistics, infrastructure, modes of deployment, force structures and exercise patterns, under conditions of increased transparency.

● A new European security equation must also comprise a residual nuclear deterrent as an ultimate guarantee of peace, with agreement on a minimum level of nuclear armament. On this point, the most recent pronouncements of Soviet spokesmen, including even Gorbachev, are encouraging.

● It is necessary to develop cooperative mechanisms to promote understanding with the East — for instance more exchanges between military academies, reciprocal troop visits, seminars to enhance shared learning.

● Comparison of NATO with the Warsaw Pact is only conceivable or useful if the latter changes fundamentally to become a voluntary alliance of free equal partners. Until this happens the two cannot properly be equated, although they often are, through thoughtlessness or for transparent reasons. Even to refer to both these alliances as military blocs is grossly misleading. The Warsaw Pact itself is no longer a bloc, let alone NATO. The Atlantic Alliance is a free association of democratic, self-determining nations of the free world, and is purely defensive in nature. Up till now the Warsaw Pact has been a military alliance lacking the legitimation of a free expression of will by the peoples involved. We hope for change, which would decisively improve the prospects for fruitful cooperation.

● Nevertheless we cannot, and will not, become guarantors of the Warsaw Pact. We are arguing neither for its dissolution nor for its continuation. Its fate will be determined by its members alone exercising free choice. This must also be allowed for in the arms control process.

● Even if the Warsaw Pact does dissolve itself that is no reason for disbanding NATO. On the contrary there is every reason to argue that our role as an agent of stability would then become even more important.

● To equate the stationing of Soviet troops in Central and Eastern Europe with the presence of American troops in Western Europe is neither acceptable nor helpful. The American and Canadian troops are here with the agreement of free parliaments and governments. The same is not true of the Soviet forces in Central and Eastern Europe — on the contrary, the free governments of Czechoslovakia and Hungary have demanded their withdrawal. Once again, the removal of Soviet troops can and indeed will lead to the reduction of American force levels, but not to a complete United States withdrawal. There are also geostrategic reasons for that. The current arms control negotiations should not be used to legitimise the presence of Soviet troops in Central and Eastern Europe against the will of the stationing countries, nor to make their withdrawal conditional on that of the North American forces.

A future European political order must build on the right of free self-determination of peoples. From the debate in the West the outlines of a European architecture for peace are already visible. It is based on existing institutions which represent the outstanding accomplishment of the post-war period:

(1) The process of European integration with its goal of political union;

(2) the Atlantic Alliance;

(3) the CSCE process.

In this context the CSCE framework for a pan-European peace system assumes special significance. The CSCE system must be extended and deepened. Such an overarching structure, however, cannot replace but only complement the Atlantic Alliance. How should a body of 35 states, which still can exercise veto rights, really guarantee security. Only the Atlantic Alliance is able to supply the structural base for the growing European architecture, to overcome crises and conflicts which can never be excluded, even with the current changes in the European landscape. The Alliance is the umbrella under which European integration is able to grow dynamically and continually. EC and CSCE would be over-burdened if they had to carry out the task of guaranteeing peace in the foreseeable time. They do not dispose of the necessary structure nor the corresponding instruments in their present and foreseeable state of evolution.

Whether we are concerned with security arrangements or a peaceful political order in Europe, we inevitably find the German question to be central.

German unity will come. We, who have striven for the triumph of democracy and for an end to the division of Europe and of Germany, must accept the crucial role of the peoples who are shaping the new order in the revolution in the East. The timetable for the achievement of German unity will not so much be determined by planners and governments as by the course of events in the GDR, as part of the tremendous restructuring of Europe, and by the free choice of the people there and in the Federal Republic. What politicians and diplomats can do is to recognise these facts and develop a framework so that the process is smooth and harmonious and avoids crises or erratic developments with the attendant risks for all of Europe.

The Alliance has been pledged to German unity since the entry of the Federal Republic in 1954/55. This is true of the three Western powers as well as of all the other Allies. The Alliance is not an obstacle to German unity, any more than it is to European integration. It helped to bring more democracy and freedom. It seeks to overcome the division of Germany and Europe. It is promoting reform in the East.

The continued existence of NATO and progress towards German unity are perfectly compatible. Indeed I would say they were mutually dependent. Now I hear sometimes: It is not realistic to assume that a reunified Germany could exist in the Atlantic Alliance. I would confront these voices with the insight drawn from our historic experience: To make the dissolution of the Alliance a *sine qua non* of German unity would deprive both Germany and Europe of a basic force for stability. Only firm anchoring in the West can provide the fundamental stability for the difficult process in which we are engaged.

A drifting, neutral Germany cannot be a solution, given the country's geostrategic position and its political, economic and military potential, and this is the view of all the Allies. It would not even be in the enlightened self-interest of the Soviets. The history of the last two centuries demonstrates this.

Thus there is no acceptable alternative to Germany remaining anchored in the Atlantic Alliance — and belonging to the European Community. Please understand that it would be a mistake to consider the German question in terms of a dynamically unfolding future while, at the same time, viewing the rôle and function of the Atlantic Alliance as merely static. The latter is another part of the same series of rapid, interdependent developments.

The Soviet Union is adapting to this movement towards German unity. Foreign Minister Shevardnadze's speech in Brussels and General Secretary Gorbachev's latest pronouncements show this. Soviet security interests and their definition have changed dramatically in the past four years. The Soviets' forward deployment in Europe since 1945 sprang partly from an expansionist drive for world power, but also from a deep-seated need for security. That need has lost its justification with the now unequivocal recognition that there is no threat from the West.

As a result, the Soviet perception of their security has changed. They no longer need a Western glacis. The Soviet Union will have to accept — and is probably already on the way to doing so — that its security will be enhanced rather than impaired by the loss of its Central and East European buffer zone. New, stable structures and increased prosperity as well as new and closer forms of international cooperation in Central and Eastern Europe will above all benefit the Soviet reform process.

The Soviet Union's security interests — in stability, freedom from threat and cooperation along the borders of the Soviet state — will be better served in the long term by the intensification of the disarmament process and the further reduction of military forces, by taking advantage of the Alliance as a cooperative partner in the management of peace, and by the extension of the CSCE system and the resulting reduction of confrontation.

In addition, special arrangements could be devised to take account of Soviet security interests with a united Germany as a member of the Atlantic Alliance.

A component of such an arrangement could be a special military status for the territory of the GDR, or perhaps an agreement not to extend military integration to that territory. These are just two possibilities out of many which could be conceived. German unity and membership of the Atlantic Alliance are perfectly compatible within a security architecture which would preserve European stability in the interest of the Soviet Union as well as of other states.

The members of the Alliance must as a matter of urgency incorporate such considerations into a common concept for progress towards German unity.

The important thing is that the European Community, the Atlantic Alliance and the CSCE should be developed as a framework for German and European unity. Omission of any of these structural elements would disrupt the balance which is so vital for the future of Germany and Europe. The Soviet Union can be sure that we take their ideas seriously, and more: we will respect their legitimate security interests.

London Declaration
on a transformed
North Atlantic Alliance

Issued by the Heads of State and Government participating in the meeting of the North Atlantic Council in London on 5-6 July 1990

1. Europe has entered a new, promising era. Central and Eastern Europe is liberating itself. The Soviet Union has embarked on the long journey toward a free society. The walls that once confined people and ideas are collapsing. Europeans are determining their own destiny. They are choosing freedom. They are choosing economic liberty. They are choosing peace. They are choosing a Europe whole and free. As a consequence, this Alliance must and will adapt.

2. The North Atlantic Alliance has been the most successful defensive alliance in history. As our Alliance enters its fifth decade and looks ahead to a new century, it must continue to provide for the common defence. This Alliance has done much to bring about the new Europe. No-one, however, can be certain of the future. We need to keep standing together, to extend the long peace we have enjoyed these past four decades. Yet our Alliance must be even more an agent of change. It can help build the structures of a more united continent, supporting security and stability with the strength of our shared faith in democracy, the rights of the individual, and the peaceful resolution of disputes. We reaffirm that security and stability do not lie solely in the military dimension, and we intend to enhance the political component of our Alliance as provided for by Article 2 of our Treaty.

3. The unification of Germany means that the division of Europe is also being overcome. A united Germany in the Atlantic Alliance of free

democracies and part of the growing political and economic integration of the European Community will be an indispensable factor of stability, which is needed in the heart of Europe. The move within the European Community towards political union, including the development of a European identity in the domain of security, will also contribute to Atlantic solidarity and to the establishment of a just and lasting order of peace throughout the whole of Europe.

4. We recognise that, in the new Europe, the security of every state is inseparably linked to the security of its neighbours. NATO must become an institution where Europeans, Canadians and Americans work together not only for the common defence, but to build new partnerships with all the nations of Europe. The Atlantic Community must reach out to the countries of the East which were our adversaries in the Cold War, and extend to them the hand of friendship.

5. We will remain a defensive alliance and will continue to defend all the territory of all of our members. We have no aggressive intentions and we commit ourselves to the peaceful resolution of all disputes. We will never in any circumstance be the first to use force.

6. The member states of the North Atlantic Alliance propose to the member states of the Warsaw Treaty Organisation a joint declaration in which we solemnly state that we are no longer adversaries and reaffirm our intention to refrain from the threat or use of force against the territorial integrity or political independence of any state, or from acting in any other manner inconsistent with the purposes and principles of the United Nations Charter and with the CSCE Final Act. We invite all other CSCE member states to join us in this commitment to non-aggression.

7. In that spirit, and to reflect the changing political role of the Alliance, we today invite President Gorbachev on behalf of the Soviet Union, and representatives of the other Central and Eastern European countries to come to Brussels and address the North Atlantic Council. We today also invite the governments of the Union of Soviet Socialist Republics, the Czech and Slovak Federal Republic, the Hungarian Republic, the Republic of Poland, the People's Republic of Bulgaria and Romania to come to NATO, not just to visit, but to establish regular diplomatic liaison with NATO. This will make it possible for

us to share with them our thinking and deliberations in this historic period of change.

8. Our Alliance will do its share to overcome the legacy of decades of suspicion. We are ready to intensify military contacts, including those of NATO Military Commanders, with Moscow and other Central and Eastern European capitals.

9. We welcome the invitation to NATO Secretary General Manfred Wörner to visit Moscow and meet with Soviet leaders.

10. Military leaders from throughout Europe gathered earlier this year in Vienna to talk about their forces and doctrine. NATO proposes another such meeting this Autumn to promote common understanding. We intend to establish an entirely different quality of openness in Europe, including an agreement on 'Open Skies'.

11. The significant presence of North American conventional and US nuclear forces in Europe demonstrates the underlying political compact that binds North America's fate to Europe's democracies. But, as Europe changes, we must profoundly alter the way we think about defence.

12. To reduce our military requirements, sound arms control agreements are essential. That is why we put the highest priority on completing this year the first treaty to reduce and limit conventional armed forces in Europe (CFE) along with the completion of a meaningful CSBM package. These talks should remain in continuous session until the work is done. Yet we hope to go further. We propose that, once a CFE Treaty is signed, follow-on talks should begin with the same membership and mandate, with the goal of building on the current agreement with additional measures, including measures to limit manpower in Europe. With this goal in mind, a commitment will be given at the time of signature of the CFE Treaty concerning the manpower levels of a unified Germany.

13. Our objective will be to conclude the negotiations on the follow-on to CFE and CSBMs as soon as possible and looking to the follow-up meeting of the CSCE to be held in Helsinki in 1992. We will seek through new conventional arms control negotiations, within the CSCE framework, further far-reaching measures in the 1990s to limit the offensive capability of conventional armed forces in Europe, so as to prevent any nation from maintaining disproportionate military

power on the continent. NATO's High Level Task Force will formulate a detailed position for these follow-on conventional arms control talks. We will make provisions as needed for different regions to redress disparities and to ensure that no one's security is harmed at any stage. Furthermore, we will continue to explore broader arms control and confidence-building opportunities. This is an ambitious agenda, but it matches our goal: enduring peace in Europe.

14. As Soviet troops leave Eastern Europe and a treaty limiting conventional armed forces is implemented, the Alliance's integrated force structure and its strategy will change fundamentally to include the following elements:

- NATO will field smaller and restructured active forces. These forces will be highly mobile and versatile so that Allied leaders will have maximum flexibility in deciding how to respond to a crisis. It will rely increasingly on multinational corps made up of national units.
- NATO will scale back the readiness of its active units, reducing training requirements and the number of exercises.
- NATO will rely more heavily on the ability to build up larger forces if and when they might be needed.

15. To keep the peace, the Alliance must maintain for the foreseeable future an appropriate mix of nuclear and conventional forces, based in Europe, and kept up to date where necessary. But, as a defensive Alliance, NATO has always stressed that none of its weapons will ever be used except in self-defence and that we seek the lowest and most stable level of nuclear forces needed to secure the prevention of war.

16. The political and military changes in Europe, and the prospects of further changes, now allow the Allies concerned to go further. They will thus modify the size and adapt the tasks of their nuclear deterrent forces. They have concluded that, as a result of the new political and military conditions in Europe, there will be a significantly reduced role for sub-strategic nuclear systems of the shortest range. They have decided specifically that, once negotiations begin on short-range nuclear forces, the Alliance will propose, in return for reciprocal action by the Soviet Union, the elimination of all its nuclear artillery shells from Europe.

17. New negotiations between the United States and the Soviet Union on the reduction of short-range nuclear forces should begin shortly after a CFE agreement is signed. The Allies concerned will develop an arms control framework for these negotiations which takes into account our requirements for far fewer nuclear weapons, and the diminished need for sub-strategic nuclear systems of the shortest range.

18. Finally, with the total withdrawal of Soviet stationed forces and the implementation of a CFE agreement, the Allies concerned can reduce their reliance on nuclear weapons. These will continue to fulfil an essential role in the overall strategy of the Alliance to prevent war by ensuring that there are no circumstances in which nuclear retaliation in response to military action might be discounted. However, in the transformed Europe, they will be able to adopt a new NATO strategy making nuclear forces truly weapons of last resort.

19. We approve the mandate given in Turnberry to the North Atlantic Council in Permanent Session to oversee the ongoing work on the adaptation of the Alliance to the new circumstances. It should report its conclusions as soon as possible.

20. In the context of these revised plans for defence and arms control, and with the advice of NATO Military Authorities and all member states concerned, NATO will prepare a new Allied military strategy moving away from 'forward defence', where appropriate, towards a reduced forward presence and modifying 'flexible response' to reflect a reduced reliance on nuclear weapons. In that connection, NATO will elaborate new force plans consistent with the revolutionary changes in Europe. NATO will also provide a forum for Allied consultation on the upcoming negotiations on short-range nuclear forces.

21. The Conference on Security and Co-operation in Europe (CSCE) should become more prominent in Europe's future, bringing together the countries of Europe and North America. We support a CSCE Summit later this year in Paris which would include the signature of a CFE agreement and would set new standards for the establishment, and preservation, of free societies. It should endorse, inter alia:

- CSCE principles on the right to free and fair elections;
- CSCE commitments to respect and uphold the rule of law;
- CSCE guidelines for enhancing economic co-operation, based on the development of free and competitive market economies; and
- CSCE co-operation on environmental protection.

22. We further propose that the CSCE Summit in Paris decide how the CSCE can be institutionalised to provide a forum for wider political dialogue in a more united Europe. We recommend that CSCE governments establish:

- a programme for regular consultations among member governments at the Heads of State and Government or Ministerial level, at least once each year, with other periodic meetings of officials to prepare for and follow up on these consultations;
- a schedule of CSCE review conferences once every two years to assess progress toward a Europe whole and free;
- a small CSCE secretariat to co-ordinate these meetings and conferences;
- a CSCE mechanism to monitor elections in all the CSCE countries, on the basis of the Copenhagen Document;
- a CSCE Centre for the Prevention of Conflict that might serve as a forum for exchanges of military information, discussion of unusual military activities, and the conciliation of disputes involving CSCE member states; and
- a CSCE parliamentary body, the Assembly of Europe, to be based on the existing parliamentary assembly of the Council of Europe, in Strasbourg, and include representatives of all CSCE member states.

The sites of these new institutions should reflect the fact that the newly democratic countries of Central and Eastern Europe form part of the political structures of the new Europe.

23. Today, our Alliance begins a major transformation. Working with all the countries of Europe, we are determined to create enduring peace on this continent.

Index